Oxford excellence for the Caribbean

GRADE 7

STP Mathematics for Jamaica

SECOND EDITION

Workbook 1

S Chandler
E Smith
I Bettison

OXFORD

Contents

 Answers to the questions in this book can be found on your support website here:
www.oxfordsecondary.com/9780198426363

1 Working with numbers

1 Which law (associative, commutative or distributive), if any, does each of these statements illustrate?

  a $5 + 3 + 7 = 7 + 3 + 5$ _____

  b $(3 \times 5) \times 2 = 3 \times (5 \times 2)$ _____

  c $7 \times 3 = 3 \times 7$ _____

  d $4 \times (2 + 5) = 4 \times 2 + 4 \times 5$

  _____

2 Write these numbers in figures:

  a forty-seven _____

  b five hundred and thirty-two _____

  c six thousand and forty _____

  d forty thousand and sixteen _____

3 Write in words:

  a 39 _____

  b 504 _____

  c 909 _____

  d 7754 _____

4 Look at the number 57 341. Write down the figure that gives:

  a the number of tens _____

  b the number of thousands _____

  c the number of hundreds _____

5 Write these numbers in order with the smallest first:

  a 27, 84, 39, 43 _____

  b 88, 17, 56, 24 _____

  c 109, 732, 909, 66, 94 _____

6 Which is the larger number, four thousand and fifty-six or four thousand and sixty-five? Write your answer in figures.

  _____

7 Use the digits 7, 4, 6 once only to write down:

  a the largest number you can make

  _____

  b the smallest number you can make.

  _____

8 Use the digits 3, 9, 0, 2 once only to write down:

  a the largest number you can make

  _____

  b the smallest number you can make.

  _____

9 Use the digits 8, 8, 6, 6 once only to write down:

  a the largest number you can make

  _____

  b the smallest number you can make.

  _____

10 Use each of the digits 4, 8, 0, 3, 5 once to write down:

  a the largest number you can make

  _____

  b the smallest number you can make.

  _____

11 Find the value of:

    a $42 + 58 + 13$ _____

    b $123 + 321 + 231$ _____

    c $59 + 221 + 73$ _____

12 Add three hundred and thirty-four, seventy-six, and sixteen.

_____

13 Find the value of:

a 47	**b** 73	**c** 64	**d** 86
+ 39	+ 55	+ 46	+ 93

e 106	**f** 534	**g** 909	**h** 429
68	95	546	333
+ 418	+ 291	+ 382	+ 777

14 Find the value of:

    a $28 + 73 + 1014$ _____

    b $309 + 722 + 4400$ _____

15 Find the value of:

$1743 + 2396 + 798$ _____

16 Do these subtractions in your head:

a 16	**b** 17	**c** 49
– 9	– 12	– 32

17 Do the following subtractions:

    a $789 – 654$ _____

    b $876 – 678$ _____

18 Take two hundred and fourteen from three hundred and thirty-nine.

_____

19 If you subtract 56 from 174 how much must you add to this answer to get 200?

_____

20 Which number is 647 nearer to, 600 or 700?

_____

21 In a street, the houses are numbered from 1 to 57.

    a How many houses have odd numbers?

    _____

    b How many houses have even numbers?

    _____

22 Write down all the pairs of numbers between 5 and 20 whose difference is 8 (for example, 9 and 17).

_____

23 Find the sum of all the even numbers between 75 and 85.

_____

24 Put + or – in each box so that the calculations are correct.

    a $14 \square 8 \square 6 = 12$

    b $8 \square 9 \square 16 \square 5 = 6$

    c $17 \square 3 \square 8 \square 4 = 24$

25 In a school with 323 students there are 15 more girls than boys. How many boys are there?

_____

26 Find the sum of all the odd numbers between 348 and 358.

_____

27 In an election 3567 voted for Andrews, 2678 voted for Chan, 762 voted for Bosley and 3225 people failed to vote. How many people were entitled to vote?

_____

28 Round each number to the nearest 100:

a 884 _____

b 542 _____

c 695 _____

d 367 _____

e 731 _____

29 Round each number to the nearest 100:

a 644 _____

b 558 _____

c 235 _____

d 896 _____

e 129 _____

30 Round each number to the nearest 50:

a 324 _____

b 572 _____

c 523 _____

d 796 _____

e 159 _____

31 Write 72 493 as an approximate number of:

a tens _____

b hundreds _____

c thousands _____

d tens of thousands. _____

32 Write each of the following numbers correct to the nearest 10:

a 474 _____

b 8483 _____

c 2046 _____

d 9995 _____

33 Write each of the following numbers correct to the nearest 100:

a 7465 _____

b 956 _____

c 3483 _____

d 8989 _____

34 Write each of the following numbers correct to the nearest 1000:

a 3775 _____

b 8009 _____

c 367452 _____

d 84528 _____

35 By writing each number correct to the nearest number of tens, find an approximate answer for:

a $340 + 285 - 457$ _____

b $54 + 28 + 33 - 85$ _____

c $242 - 201 + 66 - 88$ _____

36 Now use your calculator to find the exact answers to the calculations in question **35**. Do your estimated answers confirm that your calculated answers are probably correct?

a _____

b _____

c _____

37 Find the missing digit. It is marked with a ☐.

   a $67 - 44 = ☐3$ _____

   b $49 + 37 = ☐6$ _____

   c $83 - ☐5 = 48$ _____

   d $35 + 43 = ☐8$ _____

   e $☐7 - 62 = 25$ _____

38 Find:

   a $43 - 37 + 11 - 3$ _____

   b $56 + 71 - 87 - 13$ _____

   c $317 - 166 + 84 - 56$ _____

   d $981 - 672 + 331 - 422$ _____

39 A teacher has to mark 76 Grade 7 exercise books, 56 Grade 8 exercise books and 84 Grade 9 exercise books. What is the total number of books that the teacher has to mark?

_____

40 What is the difference in the value of the two 8s in the number 84 831?

_____

41 49 students go on a school trip. There are 5 more girls than boys. How many boys are there?

_____

42 Telegraph poles are placed at 50 metre intervals. The last pole on a stretch of road is 2150 metres from the first. How many poles are there?

_____

43 Find the difference between two thousand and sixty-seven, and nine hundred and eighty-three. Then add on fifty-four.

_____

44 Subtract two hundred and forty-seven from eleven hundred and four. Now add on forty-eight.

_____

45 Deron has 166 boxes of eggs, each of which is packed with six eggs.

   a How many eggs are there altogether in these boxes?

     _____

   b His customer wants 1000 eggs. How many eggs is he short?

     _____

46 Use each of the numbers 1 to 16 just once to complete the 4×4 magic square. Each row, column and diagonal must add up to 34.

13	1		8
	16	5	9
	7		2

47 Calculate the following divisions, giving the remainder where there is one:

   a $750 \div 100$ _____

   b $5634 \div 100$ _____

   c $644 \div 100$ _____

   d $1734 \div 100$ _____

48 Calculate the following divisions, giving the remainder where there is one:

a 573 ÷ 24 _____

b 3285 ÷ 73 _____

c 264 ÷ 36 _____

d 1945 ÷ 46 _____

49 Calculate the following divisions, giving the remainder where there is one:

a 734 ÷ 21 _____

b 3774 ÷ 37 _____

c 564 ÷ 53 _____

d 1553 ÷ 88 _____

50 Find:

a $7 + 6 \times 3 - 10$ _____

b $16 \div 4 + 8 \times 3$ _____

c $15 \div 5 + 6 \times 3 - 14$ _____

d $18 \div (11 - 2) \times 5 - 6$ _____

51 Find:

a $(9 + 3) \times (3 + 1)$ _____

b $8 \div (10 - 6) + 5$ _____

c $4 \times (9 - 5) + 3(8 - 6)$ _____

d $(10 \times 4 - 30) + 4(4 + 2)$ _____

52 Which of the numbers 6, 8, 9, 15, 30, 31, 36, 160, 169 are:

a square numbers _____

b rectangular numbers? _____

53 Write down the numbers from 5 to 15. Which of these numbers are:

a square numbers _____

b triangular numbers _____

c rectangular numbers? _____

54 Find:

a $15 \div (8 - 3)$ _____

b $3 + 4 \times (2 + 7)$ _____

c $2 \times (9 - 4) \div (8 - 3)$ _____

d $(3 + 4) \times 2 + 12 \div (7 - 3)$ _____

e $(45 - 8 + 14) \div 3$ _____

f $(55 \div 11) - (24 \div 6)$ _____

g $(21 - 13) \div (17 - 1) \times 8$ _____

55 Which is the larger, and by how much?

a 19×20 or 21×18 _____

b 14×9 or 10×13 _____

c 43×6 or 8×34 _____

d 57×7 or 43×9 _____

56 Which is the smaller, and by how much?

a 16×23 or 21×17 _____

b 15×11 or 10×16 _____

c 33×9 or 8×37 _____

d 87×7 or 72×9 _____

57 How many times can 7 be taken away from 176?

_____

58 How many times can 9 be taken away from 1200?

_____

59 My great-grandfather died on 4 June 1902 at the age of 88. His birthday was in January. In what year was he born?

_____

60 Mr Edison has 9 sets of maths textbooks with 16 books in each set, and 7 sets of science textbooks with 15 in each set.

   a How many maths textbooks does he have?

   _____

   b How many science textbooks does he have?

   _____

   c How many maths and science textbooks does he have altogether?

   _____

61 At a concert there are 58 mothers, 58 fathers, 74 single people and one child for every adult. How many people are attending the concert?

   _____

62 A bus travels 23 kilometres each hour. It takes 3 hours to travel between Keating and Camley. What distance does the bus travel?

   _____

63 Gerrard gets paid $62 550 for a five-day working week. How much is this per day?

   _____

64 Stamps of different values come in sheets of 200.

   a What is the value of a sheet of $25 stamps?

   _____

   b What is the value of a sheet of $50 stamps?

   _____

   c What is the value of a sheet of $75 stamps?

   _____

65 Frances has $1900, and buys as many ballpoint pens as she can at $45 each.

   a How many pens can she buy?

   _____

   b How much does she have left over?

   _____

66 A supporters' club hires six coaches to go to a tournament. Each coach has 53 seats and all the seats are occupied. How many supporters go to the tournament?

   _____

67 A cinema seats 650 people when full. There are 26 rows, with the same number of seats in each row. How many seats are there in each row?

   _____

68 The annual membership fee for a tennis club is $85 000 for men and $72 500 for women. How much will it cost a group of 3 men and 2 women to belong to the club for a year?

   _____

69 George has a stack of $10 000 bills that are numbered consecutively from 893 712 to 893 891. He is going to use all of them to buy a car. How much is the car?

   _____

70 In a school with 672 students, it is estimated that each student will use 18 exercise books in the course of a school year. At the beginning of the school year there are 3394 exercise books in stock. During the year the school receives two deliveries, one for 5500 and another for 4550. Estimate the number of exercise books it should have in stock at the end of the year. Give your answer correct to the nearest 50.

   _____

71 A truck owner has three trucks. One truck can carry 25 t, another can carry 15 t and the third truck can carry 10 t. Each truck makes the same number of journeys to bring 3240 t of hard core to a building site. How many journeys does each truck make?

_____

72 5000 oranges are to be packed in boxes, each box holding 64 oranges.

    a How many boxes are needed?

    _____

    b How many more oranges could be put into the last box?

    _____

73 The Redland Building Company sends out bills on the fifth of the month to be paid by the second of the following month. Excluding the day on which the bill is sent, how many days are there in which to pay a bill sent out on:

    a 5 September

    _____

    b 5 October?

    _____

    (There are 30 days in September and 31 in October.)

74 Write down the next two numbers in each sequence.

    a 4, 7, 10, 13, 16, _____

    b 20, 18, 16, 14, _____

    c 5, 9, 13, 17, _____

    d 3, 6, 12, 24, _____

    e 100, 90, 81, 73, _____

75 Write down the numbers between 18 and 30 that are:

    a square numbers _____

    b rectangular numbers _____

    c triangular numbers. _____

76 The product of three numbers is 4199.
Two of the numbers are 13 and 17.
Work out the other number.

_____

77 A service company organises a day out for its employees. Four different trips are available. The final numbers for each trip are:

Trip A: 222, Trip B: 278, Trip C: 184, Trip D: 90. The company that supplies the coaches has a fleet of 47-seater coaches.

    a How many coaches are needed altogether?

    _____

    b How many additional passengers can be taken on each trip if every seat is taken?

    Trip A _____

    Trip B _____

    Trip C _____

    Trip D _____

    c The coach operator agreed that the total cost should be worked out by calculating the fares for each person who goes on a trip as follows:

    Trip A: $3000, Trip B: $3500,

    Trip C: $2500, Trip D: $2800

    How much did the service company have to pay in total for the four trips?

    _____

d What extra income would the coach company have had if all the seats had been taken for all the trips?

_____

78 The product of three numbers is 4807. Two of the numbers are 11 and 19. Work out the other number.

_____

79 Express each of the following numbers as the product of two factors, giving all possibilities:

a 28 _____

b 42 _____

c 105 _____

80 Write down the set of multiples of:

a 4 between 15 and 30

_____

b 7 between 20 and 40

_____

c 11 between 34 and 84

_____

81 Write down the factors of 84 that are odd.

_____

82 Find a number smaller than 36 that is a multiple of 6 and 9.

_____

83 Which of the following are prime numbers?
3, 6, 9, 11, 17, 19, 21, 23

_____

84 Find a number between 80 and 90 that is a multiple of 6 and 7.

_____

85 Find the sum of all the whole numbers from 24 to 36 that are not multiples of 3.

_____

86 Which of the following are prime numbers?
27, 45, 53, 61, 71, 81

_____

87 Which of the following are not prime numbers?
29, 39, 49, 59, 69, 79

_____

88 Are the following statements true or false?

a There are five prime numbers between 4 and 20.

_____

b There are 10 prime numbers smaller than 30.

_____

c The only even prime number is 2.

_____

89 **a** Is 342 divisible by 3? _____

b Is 2923 divisible by 5? _____

c Is 364 divisible by 7? _____

90 Look at the number 10 122.

a Is it divisible by 2? _____

b Is it divisible by 3? _____

c Is it divisible by 6? _____

91 State the HCF of:

a 12, 18, 30 _____

b 25, 35, 45 _____

c 26, 39, 52 _____

d 42, 70, 98 _____

92 State the LCM of:

a 7 and 9 _____

b 3, 9 and 15 _____

c 8, 9 and 10 _____

93 Look at the numbers 31, 7, 21, 24, 13.

a Which of these numbers are:

i odd numbers _____

ii prime numbers _____

iii multiples of 3? _____

b For the largest of these numbers that is not a prime number, write down all its factors.

_____

94 Two toy cars go round a track. The first car takes 3 seconds to go round. The second car takes 5 seconds to go round. They start side by side. How long will it take before they are side by side again?

_____

95 Find the largest number of children who can equally share 126 oranges and 147 bananas.

_____

96 An exercise has 31 questions. How many questions:

a have even question numbers

_____

b have question numbers that are a multiple of 5?

_____

97 Find the largest number of children who can equally share 54 pencils and 24 pens.

_____

98 Find the least sum of money that can be divided exactly into equal amounts of $3 or $6 or $8.

_____

2 Directed numbers

1 Which temperature is higher?

    a +5° or +3°   _____

    b −5° or −3°   _____

    c −7° or −6°   _____

    d +4° or −4°   _____

2 Which temperature is lower?

    a +7° or +6°   _____

    b −4° or −5°   _____

    c −2° or −4°   _____

    d +9° or +12°   _____

    e −1° or +1°   _____

3 Use positive or negative numbers to describe the given quantities:

    a 10 seconds before the start of a race

    _____

    b 10 seconds after the start of a race

    _____

    c 14 steps up a flight of stairs

    _____

    d The deepest part of a lake that is 50 metres below the surface

    _____

    e A debt of $25

    _____

4 Use positive or negative numbers to describe the given quantities:

    a A debt of $10 000

    _____

    b One minute before the bus arrives

    _____

    c Walking ten paces backwards

    _____

    d $1000 in your pocket

    _____

5 At midday the temperature was −3 °C. At 3 pm it was 2 °C warmer. What was the temperature at 3 pm?

    _____

6 At 4 pm the temperature was 8 °C. By midnight it had dropped by 10 °C. What was the temperature at midnight?

    _____

7 Write either > or < between the two numbers:

    a 5   4   **b** −3   −1

    c −4   −8   **d** −3   −5

8 Write down the next two numbers in each sequence:

    a −6, −3, 0, _____

    b 12, 7, 2, _____

    c −3, −6, −12, _____

    d −8, −5, −2, _____

9 Find, using a number line if it helps:

    a $7 - 9$ _____

    b $-4 + 7$ _____

    c $(+3) - (+6)$ _____

    d $(+2) - (+6) + (+7)$ _____

    e $(-7) - (+4) + (+5)$ _____

10 Find, using a number line if it helps:

    a $(+4) - (+7)$ _____

    b $8 - 5 + 3$ _____

    c $8 - 3 - 6$ _____

    d $7 - 6 - 9$ _____

11 Find:

    a $5 - (3)$ _____

    b $(-4) + (-4)$ _____

    c $2 - (-6)$ _____

    d $8 + (-2) - (-2)$ _____

    e $-3 - (-3) + (-4)$ _____

    f $14 + (-12) - (-5)$ _____

12 Find:

    a $-5 + (+8) + (-5)$ _____

    b $4 + (-7) - (+2)$ _____

    c $6 - (-3) + (+6)$ _____

    d $-2 - (8 - 11)$ _____

13 **a** Subtract 6 from -5.

    _____

    b Add -4 to 3.

    _____

    c Find the value of twice negative 4.

    _____

    d Find the value of four times -3.

    _____

14 **a** Add -12 to 3.

    _____

    b Subtract 12 from 3.

    _____

    c Find the value of seven times -6.

    _____

    d Find the value of three times negative five.

    _____

15 **a** Add -4 to -5 _____

    b Subtract 8 from -4 _____

    c Subtract -3 from 9 _____

    d Add -6 to 8 _____

16 Calculate:

    a $(-2) \times (+4)$ _____

    b $7 \times (-6)$ _____

    c $-4(-3)$ _____

    d $-9(4)$ _____

    e $(+5) \times (+7)$ _____

    f $(-5) \times (-8)$ _____

17 Calculate:

    a $-15 \div 5$ _____

    b $(-24) \div (-6)$ _____

    c $-9 \div 3$ _____

    d $-12 \div 2$ _____

    e $\dfrac{24}{-3}$ _____

    f $\dfrac{-49}{7}$ _____

18 Calculate:

    a $24 + 6(7 - 5)$ _____

    b $2 + 8 \div (-4)$ _____

    c $12 - 3(1 + 3)$ _____

    d $9 - 4(2 - 4)$ _____

19 a $5 + 7 \times 4 - (6 + 11)$ _____

    b $12 + (11 \times 5 + 5) - 10$ _____

    c $27 - 4 \times 3 + 8$ _____

    d $44 \div 11 + 2 \times (9 - 5)$ _____

20 a $10 + (3 \times 8 - 3)$ _____

    b $3 \times (2 + 3 \times 9)$ _____

    c $5 \times 4 + 24 \div 8$ _____

    d $(9 - 5) \times 20 - 6 \times 2$ _____

21 a $(18 + 30 \div 6) + 4 \times 7$ _____

    b $(19 + 6) \times 7 - 45$ _____

    c $13 - 36 \div 12 + 16 \times 2$ _____

    d $(10 + 32 - 2) \div 8 + 5$ _____

In questions **22** to **36**, choose the letter that corresponds to the correct answer.

22 Which of the four temperatures is the highest?

    A $-7\,°C$ **B** $-4\,°C$

    C $0\,°C$ **D** $+7°$

23 Which of the four temperatures is the lowest?

    A $-7\,°C$ **B** $-4\,°C$

    C $0\,°C$ **D** $+7\,°C$

24 Which of the four temperatures is the highest?

    A $5°$ **B** $-5°$

    C $-8°$ **D** $3°$

25 Which of the four temperatures is the lowest?

    A $-6°$ **B** $2°$

    C $-7°$ **D** $0°$

26 The next two numbers in the sequence $-2, -4, -6$, are:

    A $-6, -8$ **B** $-8, -9$

    C $-8, -10$ **D** $-10, -12$

27 The value of $(-4) + (+5) - (-5)$ is:

    A -6 **B** -4

    C 4 **D** 6

28 The value of $-5 - (8 - 12)$ is:

    A -9 **B** -1

    C 0 **D** 1

29 If -3 is subtracted from 5, and then 6 is added to the answer, the result is:

    A -2 **B** 2

    C 10 **D** 14

30 The value of $(-7) \times (-3)$ is:

    A -21 **B** -10

    C 10 **D** 21

31 The value of $(-48 \div (-12))$ is:

    A -36 **B** -4

    C 4 **D** 36

32 The value of $3(4 - 6) + 4(10 - 8)$ is:

    A -2 **B** 0

    C 2 **D** 14

33 The value of $6(5 + 7) \div 3(13 - 7)$ is:

    A 2 **B** 3

    C 4 **D** 6

34 The value of $-3(-6)$ is:

    A -9 **B** 9

    C -18 **D** 18

35 The value of $4(-3)$ is:

    A 7 **B** 12

    C -12 **D** -7

36 The value of $3(9 - 5) \div (-2)(7 - 5)$ is:

    A 4 **B** 8

    C 3 **D** -3

3 Fractions

1 Express the first quantity as a fraction of the second:

a 45 seconds; 3 minutes

_____

b 60c; $2

_____

c 50 minutes; 2 hours

_____

d 5 days; the number of days in the month of June

_____

2 Fill in the missing numbers to make equivalent fractions:

a $\dfrac{7}{10} = \dfrac{}{50}$

b $\dfrac{4}{9} = \dfrac{}{36}$

c $\dfrac{4}{7} = \dfrac{12}{}$

d $\dfrac{2}{33} = \dfrac{}{99}$

e $\dfrac{5}{8} = \dfrac{35}{}$

3 Write each fraction as an equivalent fraction with denominator 36:

a $\dfrac{3}{4}$ _____

b $\dfrac{7}{9}$ _____

c $\dfrac{11}{12}$ _____

d $\dfrac{11}{18}$ _____

4 Which fraction is the larger?

a $\dfrac{3}{5}$ or $\dfrac{4}{7}$ _____

b $\dfrac{2}{11}$ or $\dfrac{3}{20}$ _____

c $\dfrac{5}{9}$ or $\dfrac{5}{8}$ _____

5 Put either > or < between the fractions:

a $\dfrac{3}{11}$ $\dfrac{2}{7}$

b $\dfrac{9}{11}$ $\dfrac{3}{4}$

c $\dfrac{3}{8}$ $\dfrac{5}{12}$

d $\dfrac{5}{9}$ $\dfrac{6}{11}$

6 Arrange the following fractions in ascending order:

a $\dfrac{13}{24}, \dfrac{2}{3}, \dfrac{7}{12}, \dfrac{5}{6}, \dfrac{5}{8}$ _____

b $\dfrac{2}{9}, \dfrac{7}{18}, \dfrac{1}{3}, \dfrac{5}{6}, \dfrac{4}{9}$ _____

c $\dfrac{3}{10}, \dfrac{2}{5}, \dfrac{7}{25}, \dfrac{13}{50}, \dfrac{3}{5}$ _____

d $\dfrac{3}{5}, \dfrac{7}{9}, \dfrac{11}{12}, \dfrac{3}{4}$ _____

7 Simplify the following fractions:

a $\dfrac{27}{36}$ _____

b $\dfrac{24}{42}$ _____

c $\dfrac{55}{121}$ _____

d $\dfrac{36}{84}$ _____

8 Add the fractions, simplifying the answers where you can:

a $\dfrac{7}{15} + \dfrac{8}{15}$ _____

b $\dfrac{8}{21} + \dfrac{4}{21}$ _____

c $\dfrac{9}{30} + \dfrac{7}{30}$ _____

9 Add the fractions, simplifying the answers where you can:

a $\dfrac{7}{24} + \dfrac{1}{24} + \dfrac{11}{24} + \dfrac{2}{24}$ _____

b $\dfrac{3}{13} + \dfrac{2}{13} + \dfrac{6}{13} + \dfrac{1}{13}$ _____

c $\dfrac{3}{77} + \dfrac{12}{77} + \dfrac{13}{77} + \dfrac{5}{77}$ _____

10 Find:

a $\dfrac{2}{5} + \dfrac{1}{6}$ _____

b $\dfrac{3}{10} + \dfrac{2}{3}$ _____

c $\dfrac{1}{6} + \dfrac{2}{7}$ _____

11 Add the fractions, simplifying the answers where you can:

a $\dfrac{2}{15} + \dfrac{7}{30}$ _____

b $\dfrac{2}{11} + \dfrac{5}{9}$ _____

c $\dfrac{4}{15} + \dfrac{1}{5} + \dfrac{3}{10}$ _____

d $\dfrac{5}{12} + \dfrac{1}{6} + \dfrac{1}{3}$ _____

12 Find:

a $\dfrac{9}{13} - \dfrac{4}{13}$ _____

b $\dfrac{7}{12} - \dfrac{1}{6}$ _____

c $\dfrac{23}{30} - \dfrac{1}{3} - \dfrac{2}{5}$ _____

13 Find:

a $\dfrac{11}{12} - \dfrac{5}{8} + \dfrac{1}{4}$ _____

b $\dfrac{5}{6} + \dfrac{2}{9} - \dfrac{2}{3}$ _____

c $\dfrac{1}{2} + \dfrac{3}{10} - \dfrac{57}{100}$ _____

d $\dfrac{5}{12} + \dfrac{1}{6} + \dfrac{1}{3}$ _____

14 Change these improper fractions to mixed numbers:

a $\dfrac{43}{9}$ _____

b $\dfrac{59}{7}$ _____

c $\dfrac{96}{11}$ _____

15 Change these mixed numbers to improper fractions:

a $5\frac{1}{4}$ _____

b $8\frac{3}{5}$ _____

c $12\frac{3}{7}$ _____

16 Calculate the following divisions, giving your answers as mixed numbers:

a $46 \div 11$ _____

b $31 \div 4$ _____

c $76 \div 12$ _____

17 Find:

a $5\frac{1}{3} + 2\frac{1}{6}$ _____

b $3\frac{11}{12} + 1\frac{1}{4}$ _____

c $2\frac{1}{2} + 7\frac{9}{16}$ _____

18 Find:

a $5\frac{1}{3} + 3\frac{3}{4} + 7\frac{2}{5}$ _____

b $7\frac{3}{10} + 2\frac{5}{8} + 3\frac{1}{2}$ _____

c $4\frac{5}{14} + 2\frac{4}{9} + 3\frac{2}{7}$ _____

19 Find:

a $\dfrac{3}{4} - \dfrac{2}{3}$ _____

b $\dfrac{3}{5} - \dfrac{7}{20}$ _____

c $\dfrac{3}{4} - \dfrac{1}{6} - \dfrac{2}{5}$ _____

20 Find:

a $9\frac{3}{4} - 7\frac{5}{8}$ _____

b $5\frac{7}{8} - 4\frac{3}{5}$ _____

c $12\frac{11}{16} - 7\frac{1}{2}$ _____

21 Find:

a $7\frac{1}{2} - 3\frac{2}{3}$ _____

b $6\frac{1}{4} - 1\frac{5}{8}$ _____

c $10\frac{3}{8} - 7\frac{3}{4}$ _____

22 Find:

a $5\frac{2}{5} + 4\frac{5}{6} - 6\frac{3}{4}$ _____

b $4\frac{7}{12} - 3\frac{5}{8} + 1\frac{2}{3}$ _____

c $12\frac{6}{7} - 5\frac{1}{3} - 1\frac{1}{4}$ _____

23 What must be added to $\frac{1}{3} + \frac{1}{4} + \frac{1}{5}$ to make 1?

_____

24 How much bigger than 2 is $\frac{2}{3} + \frac{5}{6} + \frac{3}{4}$?

_____

25 Which is the smaller, and by how much?

$$\frac{5}{7} - \frac{2}{3} + \frac{1}{6} \quad \text{or} \quad \frac{3}{4} - \frac{2}{7} - \frac{5}{28}$$

_____

26 Which is the larger, and by how much?

$$\frac{1}{6} + \frac{1}{8} - \frac{1}{4} \quad \text{or} \quad \frac{1}{3} - \frac{2}{9} + \frac{1}{6}$$

_____

27 A petrol storage tank is $\frac{3}{4}$ full. After a quantity of petrol is drawn off, the tank is $\frac{3}{5}$ full. What fraction of a full tank was drawn off?

_____

28 Eddy has a 2 litre tin of paint which is two-thirds full. After he has given a door one coat of paint the tin is seven-twelfths full. What fraction of the tin was needed to paint the door?

_____

29 An airline allows each passenger 22 kg of luggage. Maxine has one case of mass $9\frac{5}{6}$ kg and another of mass $7\frac{4}{9}$ kg. How many kilograms is she under the limit?

_____

30 In a class of students, half of them come by bus, two-fifths come by car and the remainder walk.

a What fraction of the students walk to school?

_____

b What fraction do not come by car?

_____

31 Of the 525 students at Weston School, $\frac{1}{3}$ travel by bus, $\frac{1}{5}$ travel by car and the rest cycle.

a What fraction of the students cycle to school?

_____

b How many students cycle to school?

_____

32 Grade 10 students have to choose one subject out of chemistry, physics, biology and geography. If $\frac{1}{5}$ choose chemistry, $\frac{1}{6}$ physics, 21 biology and $\frac{2}{5}$ geography, how many students choose:

a chemistry _____

b geography _____

c physics? _____

33 The ground around Jim's home is used as follows: $\frac{1}{8}$ of the total area for flowers; $\frac{9}{40}$ of the total area for vegetables; $\frac{5}{8}$ of the total area for grass; and 12 square metres is needed for a shed to stand on. Work out:

a the total area of the ground Jim owns

b the area he has for grass

_____

c the area used for vegetables.

_____

34 In a group of 90 boys, $\frac{1}{3}$ play football, $\frac{2}{5}$ play cricket, $\frac{1}{6}$ play both sports while the remainder play neither sport. How many boys play:

a both sports _____

b neither sport _____

c cricket? _____

35 Velma baked a cake. She gave one-sixth of it to Kevin and half of the remainder to Marcia. What fraction of the cake remains?

_____

36 A sum of money was divided between four girls. The first received one-third of it, the second two-fifths, the third one-sixth. What fraction did the fourth girl receive?

_____

37 Find:

a $\frac{5}{8} \times \frac{3}{10}$ _____

b $\frac{20}{21} \times \frac{7}{4}$ _____

c $\frac{7}{12} \times \frac{9}{28} \times \frac{4}{5}$ _____

38 Find:

a $4\frac{1}{2} \times \frac{4}{9}$ _____

b $5\frac{1}{3} \times 1\frac{3}{8}$ _____

c $1\frac{2}{5} \times 2\frac{1}{2}$ _____

39 Find:

a $2\frac{5}{8} \times \frac{3}{7} \times 2\frac{2}{5}$ _____

b $3\frac{1}{6} \times 1\frac{5}{7} \times 5\frac{1}{4}$ _____

c $3\frac{3}{7} \times 1\frac{5}{9} \times 2\frac{1}{8}$ _____

40 Find:

a $2\frac{1}{9} \times 18$ _____

b $3\frac{2}{7} \times 21$ _____

c $4 \times 3\frac{3}{8}$ _____

41 Find:

a $\frac{1}{5}$ of 45   _____

b $\frac{5}{8}$ of 40   _____

c $\frac{3}{7}$ of 77   _____

d $\frac{7}{12}$ of 84   _____

42 Find:

a $\frac{5}{7}$ of 63 litres   _____

b $\frac{4}{9}$ of 108 metres   _____

c $\frac{3}{11}$ of 99 days   _____

d $\frac{7}{8}$ of $42   _____

43 **a** How many $\frac{1}{3}$s are there in 4?

_____

b How many $\frac{3}{5}$s are there in 12?

_____

c How many $\frac{2}{5}$s are there in 8?

_____

44 Find:

a $12 \div \dfrac{4}{5}$

_____

b $27 \div \dfrac{9}{11}$

_____

c $\dfrac{14}{19} \div \dfrac{7}{2}$

_____

d $\dfrac{28}{27} \div \dfrac{4}{9}$

_____

45 Find:

a $4\frac{1}{2} \div 1\frac{1}{2}$

_____

b $6\frac{2}{5} \div 9\frac{3}{5}$

_____

c $4\frac{1}{3} \div 9\frac{3}{4}$

_____

d $5\frac{1}{3} \div 1\frac{1}{7}$

_____

46 Divide:

a $4\frac{2}{5}$ by $5\frac{1}{2}$

_____

b $2\frac{1}{3}$ by $1\frac{5}{9}$

_____

c $4\frac{1}{7}$ by $2\frac{5}{12}$

_____

47 Find:

a $5\frac{1}{3} \times 2\frac{5}{8} \div 4\frac{2}{3}$

_____

b $4\frac{2}{3} \div \frac{5}{9} \times 2\frac{1}{2}$

_____

c $3\frac{3}{7} \div 11\frac{2}{3} \times 8\frac{1}{6}$

_____

d $2\frac{1}{6}, \frac{2}{3}, 5\frac{1}{2}$

_____

48 Calculate:

a $\dfrac{3}{8} + \dfrac{3}{4} \div \dfrac{1}{2}$

_____

b $\dfrac{4}{9} \div \left(\dfrac{5}{6} - \dfrac{2}{3} \right)$

_____

c $\dfrac{3}{4} + \left(\dfrac{5}{7} \div \dfrac{3}{4} \right) \times 4\frac{1}{5}$

_____

d $\dfrac{5}{12} - \dfrac{7}{20} \times \left(\dfrac{4}{7} - \dfrac{1}{3} \right)$

_____

49 Find:

a $6\frac{1}{2} - \frac{3}{4} - 3\frac{1}{4}$

_____

b $1\frac{1}{2} + 5\frac{1}{8} - 5\frac{3}{4}$

_____

c $4\frac{1}{2} - 2\frac{1}{3} \times 1\frac{1}{2}$

_____

d $1\frac{4}{5} \div \frac{3}{4} \times 2\frac{1}{7}$

_____

50 How many $4\frac{1}{2}$ cm lengths of wire can be cut from a coil of wire that is 90 cm long?

_____

51 How many bottles of squash, each holding $\frac{7}{10}$ litre, can Sally fill from a cask holding $10\frac{1}{2}$ litres?

_____

52 In the election for the president of a club, Stewart Brown got $\frac{5}{12}$ of the votes and Mike Tippett got $\frac{1}{2}$ the votes. 12 members decided not to vote.

  a What fraction of the members:

   i voted

   _____

   ii did not vote?

   _____

  b How many members are in the club?

   _____

  c How many votes did the winner receive?

   _____

53 My school is divided into lower school, middle school and upper school. $\frac{1}{4}$ of the students are in upper school, $\frac{2}{5}$ in middle school and 301 in lower school.

  a What fraction of the students are in lower school?

   _____

  b How many students are there in the school?

   _____

54 A Member of Parliament holds a monthly meeting for his constituents. The meeting lasts for two hours. He estimates that he needs to allow five minutes for each constituent.

  a What fraction of the total time is allowed for each constituent?

   _____

  b How many constituents should he be able to see in the scheduled time?

   _____

  c Last month 26 constituents turned up to see him. What fraction of constituents were unable to see him?

   _____

55 A fuel storage tank is three-quarters full. After 75 litres have been drained out, the tank is three-fifths full. What is the capacity of the tank?

   _____

56 One-fifth of the seats for a concert cost $4500, one-third cost $3000 and the remainder cost $2000.

  a What fraction of the seats cost $2000?

   _____

  b If there are 210 seats at $2000, how many people can be seated altogether?

   _____

57 The local council agrees to pay $\frac{3}{7}$ of the cost of running a leisure centre, with central government paying the remainder. If the local council pays $420 000, find the total running cost.

   _____

58 A cricket club consists of eight members who are good batsmen only, seven who are good bowlers only, five are all-rounders and there are some non-players. If there are 30 members in the club, what fraction of them are:

a non-players

_____

b good bowlers only

_____

c all-rounders?

_____

59 Sonia read 20 pages of her book in half an hour.

a How many minutes does it take her to read:

i one page

_____

ii 36 pages?

_____

b She is able to read the whole book in $5\frac{1}{2}$ hours. How many pages are there in the book?

_____

60 A doctor estimates that it takes him $3\frac{1}{2}$ minutes to see a patient in his surgery.

a How many patients does he expect to see in his morning surgery, which lasts $1\frac{3}{4}$ hours?

_____

b Evening surgery is time-tabled to last $1\frac{1}{4}$ hours. Twenty patients attend to see him. Should he be able to see all of them in $1\frac{1}{4}$ hours? Justify your answer.

_____

61 In a local election there were two candidates. Allan Southland got $\frac{5}{12}$ of the votes and Betty Curtis got $\frac{1}{3}$ of the votes. A total of 3000 who were entitled to vote did not do so.

a What fraction of the electorate

i voted _____

ii did not vote? _____

b How large was the electorate?

_____

c How many votes did Betty Curtis get?

_____

62 In a business the total receipts for the year were used as follows:

$\frac{2}{5}$ was spent on materials, $\frac{7}{20}$ on wages, $\frac{1}{10}$ on fixed overheads, $\frac{1}{20}$ on dividends, and the remainder was put into the reserve fund.

a What fraction of the income was placed in the reserve fund?

_____

b If $350 million was placed in the reserve fund, how much was spent on:

i materials

_____

ii wages?

_____

4 Decimals

1 What is the value of the digit 4 in each of the following numbers? The first one has been done for you.

   a 34.7   _4 units_

   b 65.4   _____

   c 48.2   _____

   d 85.04   _____

2 Write these numbers in order of size with the smallest number first.

   a 7.6, 7.06, 7.77

   _____

   b 31.72, 37.21, 32.17, 31.27

   _____

   c 9.42, 9.14, 9.24, 9.22

   _____

3 Write these decimals as fractions.

   a 0.83 _____

   b 0.41 _____

   c 0.013 _____

   d 0.0071 _____

   e 0.0211 _____

4 Write these decimals as fractions in their lowest terms.

   a 0.75 _____

   b 0.8 _____

   c 0.64 _____

   d 0.0035 _____

   e 0.16 _____

5 Write these decimals as fractions in their lowest terms.

   a 0.0405 _____

   b 0.375 _____

   c 0.055 _____

   d 0.0066 _____

6 **a** How many tenths must be added to 7.3 to make a total of 8?

   _____

   b How many hundredths must be added to 4.48 to make a total of 5?

   _____

   c How many tenths must be added to 16.8 to make 19?

   _____

   d How many hundredths must be subtracted from 2.77 to make 2?

   _____

7 Write the following as decimals:

   a $\frac{9}{100}$ _____

   b $\frac{17}{100}$ _____

   c $3\frac{7}{10}$ _____

   d $9\frac{31}{1000}$ _____

   e $8\frac{7}{10}$ _____

8 Find:

a 4.72 + 1.26

_____

b 0.15 + 0.15

_____

c 8.2 + 0.004

_____

d 3.45 + 0.742

_____

e 0.64 + 0.064 + 0.006

_____

9 Find:

a 10 − 7.2 _____

b 8.6 − 5.4 _____

c 6.92 − 1.09 _____

d 105.7 − 58.6 _____

e 7.5 − 2.92 _____

f 0.03 − 0.000 71 _____

g 9 − 0.007 36 _____

10 Find:

a 4.724 − 1.936 _____

b 64.08 − 13.63 _____

c 14.33 − 0.37 _____

d 204.7 − 165.8 _____

11 Find:

a 5.94 + 7.26 − 8.3 _____

b 17.3 − 4.92 − 5.87 _____

c 54.2 − 18.9 − 23.2 _____

d 79.3 − 8.245 − 36.08 _____

12 Find:

a 5.4 − 2.6 + 8.5 _____

b 1.3 + 13 − 0.13 _____

c 86 − 3.45 − 17.2 _____

d 5.6 + 0.33 − 4.008 _____

e 3.7 − 0.043 + 5.9 _____

f 80 − 45.21 − 19.66 _____

g 2.05 + 3.007 − 1.88 _____

13 One book costs $449.90 and another costs $379.50.

a How much do the two books cost together?

_____

b How much change should I get if I pay with a $1000 bill?

_____

14 a Find the total cost of three articles costing $45, $137.55 and $168.45.

_____

b I pay with two $200 bills. How much change do I get?

_____

15 Add 15.4 to 7.03 and subtract their total from 30.

_____

16 What is the perimeter of this quadrilateral?

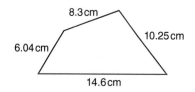

21

17 The perimeter of this triangle is 30 cm. Work out the length of the third side.

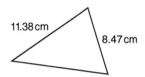

_____

18 The diagram shows the measurements of a garden, which is fenced all the way around. The lengths of three of the sides are shown. If the perimeter of the garden is 180 m, find the length of the fourth side.

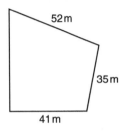

_____

19 Find the value of:

a 26.44 × 100 _____

b 0.033 × 10 _____

c 2 ÷ 100 _____

d 0.7 ÷ 1000 _____

e 0.055 × 100 _____

f 14 ÷ 10 000 _____

20 Calculate the following products:

a 0.04 × 0.5 _____

b 4 × 0.4 _____

c 0.7 × 0.006 _____

d 0.006 × 0.003 _____

21 Calculate the following products:

a 5.6 × 0.2 _____

b 39 × 0.32 _____

c 0.13 × 14 _____

d 1.8 × 8.1 _____

e 7.3 × 5.6 _____

22 Find the cost of 100 articles at $247 each.

_____

23 Wall tiles are 0.45 cm thick. How tall is a stack of 24 tiles?

_____

24 Find the value of:

a 614.3 ÷ 100 _____

b 87 ÷ 10 _____

c 4.21 ÷ 1000 _____

d 0.0005 ÷ 100 _____

25 Divide 5.7 by 1000 and multiply the result by 10.

_____

26 Subtract 0.7 from 3 and multiply the result by 100.

_____

27 Take 0.26 from 1.55 and divide the result by 100.

_____

28 Find the value of:

a 1.8 ÷ 6 _____

b 27.5 ÷ 5 _____

c 0.0028 ÷ 4 _____

d 292 ÷ 8 _____

e 0.0618 ÷ 6 _____

29 Find the value of:

   a   40.5 ÷ 15 _____

   b   77.4 ÷ 43 _____

   c   81.6 ÷ 17 _____

   d   7.28 ÷ 14 _____

   e   15.4 ÷ 28 _____

30 The perimeter of a square is 9.64 cm. What is the length of one side?

_____

31 The perimeter of a regular pentagon (a shape with five equal sides) is 18.5 cm. Work out the length of one side.

_____

32 Divide $398.58 equally between seven students.

_____

33 Express the following numbers as decimals:

   a $\dfrac{3}{4}$ _____

   b $\dfrac{9}{16}$ _____

   c $7\dfrac{3}{5}$ _____

   d $\dfrac{3}{32}$ _____

   e $\dfrac{35}{4}$ _____

   f $\dfrac{16}{5}$ _____

34 Divide 63 by 15.

_____

35 Divide 0.34 by ten thousand.

_____

36 Express $\dfrac{5}{16}$ as a decimal.

_____

37 Divide 3.5 by 25.

_____

38 Express 5.016 as a mixed number with a fraction in its lowest terms.

_____

39 My electricity bill for lighting and air conditioning was $32 400. If $\dfrac{7}{9}$ of the cost was for air conditioning, how much did I pay for lighting?

_____

40 The sum of two adjacent sides of a square is 14.7 cm.

   a   What is the length of one side?

_____

   b   What is the perimeter of this square?

_____

41 Sarah has $2450 in her purse. She buys two articles costing $895 each and one article costing $575. How much remains after this transaction?

_____

42 The perimeter of a regular octagon is 27.6 cm. What is the length of one side?

_____

43 From a plank of wood 5 metres long, Davian cuts one piece 1.8 metres long and another piece 2.46 metres long. What length remains?

_____

44 Natalie has a large bag of rice. She takes out 0.375 kg for a recipe, and then gives half of what's left to her sister. Now the bag contains 4.3 kg of rice. How much rice did the bag contain to start with?

_____

45 a Find the cost of 10 toys at $235.50 each.

_____

b Multiply 2.8 by 6 and divide the result by 7.

_____

c Find the perimeter of a regular pentagon with side lengths of 3.45 cm.

_____

46 a Divide 27.3 kg into 7 equal parts.

_____

b Find the cost of 4.5 metres of material at $146.50 per metre.

_____

47 A fence 48 metres long is to be built along one side of a vegetable garden. Clive puts in 17 posts which are equally spaced. What is the distance between neighbouring posts?

_____

48 Find, giving exact answers:

a 0.84×0.4 _____

b 3.47×0.7 _____

c 13.4×0.6 _____

d 9.2×0.03 _____

49 Find, giving exact answers:

a 1.72×0.5 _____

b 0.56×0.8 _____

c 22.3×0.06 _____

d 8.4×0.02 _____

50 A truck has a mass of 2.54 tonnes. It is loaded with 30 boxes, each box having a mass of 0.046 tonnes. Find:

a the total mass of the boxes

_____

b the total mass of the loaded lorry.

_____

51 Tablets each have a mass of 0.54 grams. They are packed into foil strips. Each strip contains 24 tablets. Each box holds four foil strips. 250 boxes are packed into a carton. What is the mass of the tablets in a carton?

_____

52 If I give 0.35 of my collection of stamps to my brother and half of the remainder to my friend Phil, I still have 390 stamps. How many stamps did I have to begin with?

_____

53 Find the value of:

a $4.29 \div 3$ _____

b $1.26 \div 7$ _____

c $0.0024 \div 6$ _____

d 0.05×0.06 _____

e 3×0.007 _____

f 9×0.06 _____

54 Find the value of:

a 1.8×0.4 _____

b $108.8 \div 17$ _____

c 0.17×0.17 _____

d 140×0.04 _____

e $50.4 \div 36$ _____

f $39.48 \div 94$ _____

55 Find the value of:

a $3.9 \div 0.3$ _____

b 1.6×0.8 _____

c 0.4×0.8 _____

d $43.2 \div 3.6$ _____

e $126 \div 0.07$ _____

f $61.5 \div 75$ _____

56 Give the following numbers correct to the nearest whole number:

a 34.6 _____   **b** 9.79 _____

c 5.858 _____   **d** 6.734 _____

57 Give the following numbers correct to three decimal places:

a 0.7649 _____   **b** 0.05936 _____

c 2.8888 _____   **d** 0.47474 _____

58 Give the following numbers correct to two decimal places:

a 1.3457 _____   **b** 0.0589 _____

c 26.9267 _____   **d** 53.625 _____

59 Give the following numbers correct to the number of decimal places indicated in the brackets:

a 52.56 (1) _____   **b** 1.839 (1) _____

c 1.839 (nearest whole number) _____

d 1.839 (2) _____

e 0.000839 (4) _____

f 78.454 (1) _____

60 Give the following numbers correct to the number of decimal places indicated in the brackets:

a 176.447 (2) _____

b 49.33 (1) _____

c 0.000728 (4) _____

d 7.6305 (3) _____

e 82.66 (1) _____

f 3.5043 (nearest whole number) _____

61 Calculate, giving your answer correct to two decimal places:

a $0.724 \div 3$ _____

b $3.142 \div 9$ _____

c $18.56 \div 5$ _____

d $0.7634 \div 7$ _____

62 Calculate, giving your answer correct to one decimal place:

a $42.6 \div 7$ _____

b $16.1 \div 15$ _____

c $524 \div 34$ _____

d $478.3 \div 28$ _____

63 Calculate, giving your answer correct to three decimal places:

a $0.4293 \div 19$ _____

b $0.98 \div 33$ _____

c $1.37 \div 12$ _____

d $1.25 \div 13$ _____

64 Find the exact answer to these calculations:

    a $0.231 \div 0.11$ _____

    b $0.088 \div 0.16$ _____

    c $0.1263 \div 0.03$ _____

    d $0.3948 \div 0.047$ _____

65 Find the value of:

    a $\dfrac{1.6}{2 \times 0.4}$ _____

    b $\dfrac{2.4 \times 0.4}{0.6}$ _____

    c $\dfrac{55 \times 8}{11}$ _____

    d $\dfrac{3.5 \times 0.9}{6.3}$ _____

66 Express these fractions as decimals and then write them in order with the smallest first.

    a $\dfrac{3}{5}, \dfrac{5}{8}, \dfrac{9}{16}$ _____

    b $\dfrac{31}{100}, \dfrac{19}{25}, \dfrac{1}{4}$ _____

    c $\dfrac{2}{5}, \dfrac{9}{20}, \dfrac{3}{8}$ _____

    d $\dfrac{3}{4}, \dfrac{71}{100}, \dfrac{18}{25}$ _____

67 **a** Give $\frac{3}{7}$ as a recurring decimal.

    _____

    b Find $5.9 + 0.59 + 0.0059 + 0.000\,59$.

    _____

    c Which is smaller, $\frac{5}{9}$ or 0.56?

    _____

    d Express 0.06 as a fraction in its lowest terms.

_____

In questions **68** to **76**, choose the letter that gives the correct answer.

68 The decimal 5.888 correct to two decimal places is:

  A 5.8   **B** 5.88

  C 5.89   **D** 5.9

69 When 0.079 is multiplied by 1000 the result is:

  A 0.79   **B** 7.9

  C 79   **D** 790

70 Which is the largest of these numbers?

  A $3\frac{3}{4}$ **B** 3.7

  C $3\frac{10}{13}$ **D** $3\frac{4}{5}$

71 Which is the smallest of these numbers?

  A 5.3   **B** $5\frac{5}{9}$

  C $5\frac{1}{4}$ **D** 5.35

72 When 50.6 is divided by 1000 the result is:

  A 0.0506   **B** 0.506

  C 5.06   **D** 0.005\,06

73 Which is the smallest of these numbers?

  A 3.43   **B** $3\frac{1}{3}$

  C 3.33   **D** $3\frac{3}{7}$

74 Which is the largest of these numbers?

  A 4.66   **B** $4\frac{4}{7}$

  C 4.67   **D** $4\frac{2}{3}$

75 The perimeter of this rectangle is 18.2 cm.

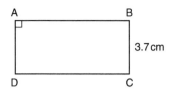

3.7 cm

The length of AB is:

A 4.4 cm   **B** 4.7 cm

C 5.4 cm   **D** 5.3 cm

76 The perimeter of this quadrilateral is 22.9 cm.

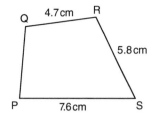

The length of PQ is:

A 4.6 cm   **B** 4.7 cm

C 4.75 cm   **D** 4.8 cm

5   Percentages

1 Express each percentage as a fraction in its lowest terms:

a 40% _____   **b** 60% _____

c 45% _____   **d** 20% _____

e 54% _____   **f** 72% _____

g $66\frac{2}{3}$% _____   **h** $82\frac{1}{2}$% _____

i $12\frac{1}{2}$% _____   **j** $10\frac{2}{3}$% _____

k 180% _____   **l** 250% _____

2 Express the following percentages in decimals giving answers correct to 3 decimal places where necessary:

a 53% _____   **b** 18% _____

c 155% _____   **d** $37\frac{3}{4}$% _____

e $41\frac{1}{8}$% _____   **f** $14\frac{1}{4}$% _____

g $3\frac{5}{8}$% _____   **h** $42\frac{4}{7}$% _____

3 Express the following fractions as percentages:

a $\frac{1}{4}$ _____   **b** $\frac{9}{10}$ _____

c $\frac{17}{20}$ _____   **d** $\frac{23}{40}$ _____

e $\frac{5}{8}$ _____   **f** $\frac{43}{60}$ _____

g $\frac{33}{25}$ _____   **h** $\frac{8}{7}$ _____

4 Express the following decimals as percentages:

a 0.75 _____   **b** 0.44 _____

c 0.38 _____   **d** 1.64 _____

e 0.535 _____   **f** 0.005 _____

g 0.175 _____   **h** 5.421 _____

5 Complete the following table:

Fraction	Percentage	Decimal
$3\frac{1}{2}$		
	40%	
		0.85
$\frac{7}{40}$		
	64%	
		0.24

6 If 83% of the students in a school have a cell phone, what percentage do not?

_____

7 In a class, 37% of the students study metalwork. What percentage do not?

_____

8 If 76% of the cost of a litre of gas is tax, what percentage is the actual cost of the gas?

_____

9 A cricket team won 55% of their matches and drew 12%. What percentage did they lose?

_____

10 The winning team in a basketball league drew 12.5% of their matches and lost 5%. What percentage of their matches did they win?

_____

11 In a school, 43% of the students study only Spanish and 39% study only French. If 13% study both languages, what percentage do not study either language?

_____

12 The cost of running a car is 28% fuel, 35% road tax, insurance and repairs. The remainder is depreciation. What percentage accounts for depreciation?

_____

13 A make of jam contains 45% fruit, 38% sugar and the remainder is water. Find the percentage of the jam that is water.

_____

14 Express the first quantity as a percentage of the second:

a 4, 40   _____

b 50, 75   _____

c 12 cm, 60 cm   _____

d 243 mm, 30 cm   _____

e 1400 g, 2 kg   _____

f 2.64 kg, 8.8 kg   _____

g 5 ft, 20 ft   _____

h 4 oranges, 5 oranges   _____

i 65 cm, 2 m   _____

j 850 m, 2 km   _____

k 66 cm^2, 99 cm^2 _____

l 3 bananas, 9 bananas   _____

m 83c, $2   _____

15 Express the second quantity as a percentage of the first:

a 10 cm, 4 cm   _____

b 5 coconuts, 3 coconuts   _____

c 1.2 m, 28 cm   _____

d 2 m, 844 mm   _____

e 450 g, $157\frac{1}{2}$ g _____

f 1 kg, 750 g   _____

g 20, 60   _____

h 60, 20   _____

i 25, 50   _____

j 10 litres, 12 litres   _____

k 76 cm, 190 mm   _____

l 8.5 t, 1.87 t   _____

m $56, 336c   _____

16 Find the value of:

a 30% of 6 m   _____

b 65% of 5 kg   _____

c 55% of 460 cm^2 _____

d 76% of 1350 km   _____

e 32% of 450 mm^2 _____

f 96% of 55 000   _____

g 85% of 2.5 km   _____

h $12\frac{1}{2}$% of 720 m _____

i $66\frac{2}{3}$% of 336 g _____

j $37\frac{1}{2}$% of 16 litres _____

k $5\frac{1}{4}$% of $5600   _____

l $33\frac{1}{3}$% of $66   _____

m $\frac{3}{4}$% of $2000   _____

17 In a history test Arlene scored 26 out of 40.

What percentage is this? _____

18 In a class of thirty-six, 75% of the students are boys.

a How many boys are there?

_____

b How many girls are there?

_____

19 In a population of 12 500, 55% are males. How many are females?

_____

20 a Express 50% as a fraction. _____

   b If 50% of a number is 30, what is the number?

_____

21 a Express 20% as a fraction. _____

   b If 20% of a number is 13, find the number.

_____

22 a Express 60% as a fraction. _____

   b If 60% of a sum of money is $984, find the sum of money.

_____

23 In an election 40% voted for Fisher, 35% voted for Morgan and 15% voted for Pigeon. If 2500 people were entitled to vote, how many:

   a voted for Fisher   _____

   b voted for Pigeon   _____

   c failed to vote?   _____

24 On a particular day, of the 600 workers in a factory, $3\frac{1}{2}$% were absent due to illness. How many of the employees were ill?

_____

25 A textbook has 350 pages of which 30% have only pictures, 10% have only tables and 6% have both tables and pictures. How many pages have:

   a pictures   _____

   b only tables   _____

   c just plain text?   _____

26 Last year Jamaica received 472 000 tourists. 29% of these came from the UK, 26% from the USA and 12% from Canada. How many tourists:

   a came from Canada   _____

   b came from the UK   _____

   c came from a country other than the three countries named above?

_____

27 The religious persuasion of the people living in St Vincent and the Grenadines is: Anglican 42%, Roman Catholic 19%, Methodist 20%, Other 19%. If 111 000 live on these islands, how many are:

   a Anglican   _____

   b Methodist   _____

   c neither Anglican nor Roman Catholic?

_____

28 The annual cost of insuring a motorbike is 7% of its purchase price. I paid $460 000 for my motorbike. How much will it cost to insure it for:

   a one year   _____

   b three years?   _____

29 In the end of term exams, Peggy scored 704 out of a possible 800.

   a What percentage was this?

_____

   b How many more marks would Peggy have needed to get 90% of the available marks?

_____

30 A packet of cereal was full when it left the factory but 'settling' caused the volume taken by the cereal to be reduced by 8%. If the volume was 3000 cm³, find the volume of the cereal after it had settled.

_____

31 In an auction, Joe sells a piece of furniture for $75 500. The auctioneer deducts 12% of the sale price as his commission.

a Work out the commission.

_____

b How much does Joe get for his piece of furniture?

_____

32 Sabina bought a coat in a sale. It was marked $25 000 but she managed to get a reduction of 40%.

a How much was the reduction?

_____

b Express the price Sabina paid as a percentage of the marked price.

_____

33 In a family, 40% of the children are boys. What is the smallest number of children that could be girls?

_____

34 In a maths test, Andrew scored 28 out of 40. What percentage was this?

_____

35 In a population of 37 500, 45% are females.

a How many males are there?

_____

b How many more males than females are there?

_____

36 The population of a town is 3440. Over the next 5 years it is expected to decrease by 15%. What size is the population expected to be in 5 years time?

_____

37 Out of 60 workers who applied to a company for employment, 36 were offered a position. What percentage was this?

_____

38 As a result of using Bettermix fertilizer, my crop of green vegetables increased by 35% compared with last year. I grew 120 kg of green vegetables last year. What mass of greens did I grow this year?

_____

39 The water rates due on Emmanuel's property this year are 8% more than they were last year. Last year he paid $88 500. What must he pay this year?

_____

40 Thomas Angel was 125 kg when he decided to go on a diet. He lost 10% of his mass in the first month and a further 8% of his original mass in the second month. What was his mass after two months of dieting?

_____

In questions **41** to **50**, choose the letter that gives the correct answer.

41 Expressed as a percentage, $5\frac{1}{4}$ is:

A 525% **B** 52.5%

C 5.25% **D** 53%

42 Expressed as a percentage, $\frac{7}{8}$ is:

A 70% **B** 78%

C 84% **D** $87\frac{1}{2}$%

43 In its lowest terms, 28% expressed as a vulgar fraction is:

A $\frac{28}{50}$ **B** $\frac{7}{25}$

C $\frac{7}{50}$ **D** $\frac{14}{50}$

44 $18000 expressed as a percentage of $40000 is:

    A 34%   **B** 40%

    C 45%   **D** 48%

45 85% of 540 m is:

    A 383 m   **B** 444 m

    C 454 m   **D** 459 m

46 Expressed as a percentage, $1\frac{3}{8}$ correct to the nearest whole number is:

    A 37%   **B** 137%

    C 138%   **D** 140%

47 Expressed as a fraction, $87\frac{1}{2}$% in its lowest terms is:

    A $\dfrac{11}{12}$ **B** $\dfrac{7}{8}$

    C $\dfrac{14}{16}$ **D** $1\frac{7}{8}$

48 Expressed as a percentage, 0.665 is:

    A 65%   **B** $66\frac{1}{2}$%

    C 67%   **D** 665%

49 Expressed as a percentage, 0.047 is:

    A 47%   **B** 5%

    C 4.7%   **D** 8%

50 34 m expressed as a percentage of 86 m, correct to the nearest whole number, is:

    A 38%   **B** 39%

    C 40%   **D** 42%

Review test 1: units 1 to 5

1 **a** Simplify $\dfrac{5}{12} \div \dfrac{15}{4}$

_____

b Express $\frac{9}{25}$ as a decimal.

_____

2 It is given that $17\,290 = 2 \times 5 \times 7 \times 13 \times 19$

a Does 19 divide exactly into 17 290? Why?

_____

b Does 49 divide exactly into 17 290? Why?

_____

c Does 38 divide exactly into 17 290? Why?

_____

3 Write down as many different three-digit numbers as you can using the digits 4, 5 and 6 once each. Put these numbers in order with the smallest first.

_____

4 Write down as many different three-digit numbers as you can using the digits 6, 7 and 9 once each. Put these numbers in order with the smallest first.

_____

5 Using all the digits 7, 0, 2, once in each number, write down:

a the largest number you can make _____

b the smallest number you can make _____

c the difference between them. _____

6 At the beginning of the day a library had 5637 books. During the day 623 books went out on loan and 774 were returned. How many books were there in the library at the end of the day?

_____

7 Find:

a 1014×78 _____

b $1014 \div 78$ _____

c $1014 + 78$ _____

d $1014 - 78$ _____

8 Find:

a $15 \times 4 + 12 \div (9 - 5)$

_____

b $15 + 4 - 12 \div (9 - 5)$

_____

c $15 - 4 - 12 + (9 - 5)$

_____

d $15 - 4 + 12 \times (9 + 5)$

_____

9 A book has 96 pages. Pages 47 to 62 are photographs. The remaining pages are all text, each of which has 38 lines with, on average, 13 words in each line.

a How many pages are just for photographs?

_____

b How many pages are all text?

_____

c On average, how many words are there on a page of text?

_____

d Ken says that the book contains about 40 000 words. Is he correct? Give a reason for your answer.

_____

10 In a class of 32 students, 12 take chemistry only, 8 take biology only, 10 take physics only, while the remainder take none of these subjects. What fraction of the class:

   a takes physics _____

   b takes chemistry or biology _____

   c does not take any of the named subjects?

   _____

11 From the numbers 0.33, $\frac{1}{3}$, $\frac{6}{17}$, $\frac{7}{20}$, 0.303, write down:

   a the largest number _____

   b the smallest number. _____

12 It is given that $48\,510 = 2 \times 3 \times 3 \times 5 \times 7 \times 7 \times 11$

   a Does 9 divide exactly into $48\,510$? Why?

   _____

   b Does 11 divide exactly into $48\,510$? Why?

   _____

   c Does 13 divide exactly into $48\,510$? Why?

   _____

   d Does 23 divide exactly into $48\,510$? Why?

   _____

13 Write $45\,926$ correct as:

   a an approximate number of tens

   _____

   b an approximate number of hundreds

   _____

   c an approximate number of thousands

   _____

   d an approximate number of tens of thousands.

   _____

14 By writing each number correct to the nearest number of tens, find an approximate answer for:

   a $436 - 248 + 64$

   _____

   b $89 - 37 + 64 - 56$

   _____

   c $932 - 674 + 52 - 78$

   _____

   d $255 - 199 + 44 - 57$

   _____

15 Find:

   a $(5 + 4) \times (7 - 3)$

   _____

   b $12 \div (9 - 5) + 2(7 - 4)$

   _____

   c $7 \times (13 - 8) - 3(10 - 6)$

   _____

   d $(8 \times 3 - 20) \div (5 + 3)$

   _____

16 Which of the numbers from 10 to 21 inclusive are:

   a square numbers

   _____

   b rectangular numbers?

   _____

17 The product of three numbers is 5083. Two of the numbers are 13 and 17. What is the third number?

   _____

18 Find, using a number line if it helps,

a $-7 + (-3) - (-4)$

_____

b $(-3) \times (6)$

_____

c $(-18) \div (-6)$

_____

19 Calculate:

a $36, 4' (9 - 4)$

_____

b $16 + 88, 11 - 9$

_____

c $3' (7 - 3), 2' (11 - 3)$

_____

20 Which of the four temperatures $+10\,°C$, $-7\,°C$, $4\,°C$, $-3\,°C$ is:

a the highest _____

b the lowest? _____

21 Put either > or < between the following pairs of fractions.

a $\frac{6}{11}$ $\frac{5}{9}$

b $\frac{7}{12}$ $\frac{2}{3}$

c $\frac{7}{12}$ $\frac{8}{15}$

22 Find:

a $\frac{4}{5} + \frac{5}{6}$ _____

b $\frac{3}{11} + \frac{4}{9}$ _____

c $\frac{7}{12} + \frac{2}{3} + \frac{5}{6}$ _____

23 Change these improper numbers into mixed numbers.

a $\frac{47}{8}$ _____

b $\frac{23}{13}$ _____

c $\frac{17}{12}$ _____

24 Fill in the missing numbers to make equivalent fractions:

a $\frac{3}{7} = \frac{12}{}$ **b** $\frac{5}{9} = \frac{}{45}$

c $\frac{2}{31} = \frac{8}{}$ **d** $\frac{7}{8} = \frac{35}{}$

25 Arrange the following fractions in ascending order:

$\frac{11}{25}, \frac{2}{5}, \frac{7}{10}, \frac{23}{50}, \frac{9}{10}$

_____

26 Change these mixed numbers into improper numbers.

a $4\frac{2}{3}$ _____

b $5\frac{3}{8}$ _____

c $11\frac{4}{9}$ _____

27 Giving each answer as a mixed number, find:

a $31 \div 6$ _____

b $75 \div 12$ _____

c $29 \div 3$ _____

28 Find:

   a $6\frac{2}{3}+1\frac{5}{6}$ _____

   b $7\frac{3}{4}-2\frac{5}{8}$ _____

29 What must be added to $\frac{2}{5}+\frac{1}{8}+\frac{5}{12}$ to make 1?

_____

30 Paula has a bag of sweets. She gives one-fifth of them to Helen and half the remainder to Tim. What fraction of the bag of sweets remains?

_____

31 Write these decimals as fractions:

   a 0.001 _____

   b 0.42 _____

   c 0.375 _____

32 Find:

   a $3.67 + 0.74$ _____

   b $23.66 + 6.19$ _____

   c $5.43 + 3.77 + 16.8$ _____

33 Find:

   a $9.26 - 7.33$ _____

   b $57.31 - 27.88$ _____

   c $0.06 - 0.00467$ _____

34 Find:

   a 83.7×100 _____

   b 0.64×100 _____

   c 0.0078×1000 _____

35 Share $46 500 equally amongst ten people.

_____

36 Find the cost of 100 articles at $4880 each.

_____

37 Find the value of:

   a $0.86 \div 2$ _____

   b $8.88 \div 3$ _____

   c $7.45 \div 5$ _____

   d $24.15 \div 7$ _____

38 Find the value of:

   a $3.52 \div 22$ _____

   b $213.4 \div 11$ _____

   c $10.58 \div 23$ _____

   d $3.015 \div 45$ _____

39 Calculate the following products:

   a 0.004×60 _____

   b 13.2×2.8 _____

   c 0.074×0.44 _____

   d 0.3745×550 _____

40 a The perimeter of a square is 36.8 cm. What is the length of a side of this square?

_____

   b If a rope which is 333 m long is cut into nine equal pieces, how long is each piece?

_____

   c The length of a side of a polygon with seven equal sides is 4.56 cm. What is the total distance around the polygon?

_____

41 Express the following fractions as decimals:

a $\dfrac{4}{25}$ _____

b $\dfrac{7}{8}$ _____

c $\dfrac{19}{32}$ _____

d $\dfrac{9}{15}$ _____

42 Express the following fractions as decimals:

a $\dfrac{7}{12}$ _____

b $\dfrac{7}{15}$ _____

c $\dfrac{2}{7}$ _____

d $\dfrac{5}{11}$ _____

43 Give the following numbers correct to three decimal places:

a 1.7564 _____

b 0.0499 _____

c 0.00057 _____

d 32.5756 _____

44 Give the following numbers correct to the number of decimal places indicated in brackets:

a 2.856 (2) _____

b 42.676 (1) _____

c 9.03606 (3) _____

d 0.06299 (4) _____

45 Calculate, giving your answers correct to two decimal places:

a 5.436 ÷ 21 _____

b 0.652 ÷ 7 _____

c 4.237 ÷ 9 _____

d 19.65 ÷ 26 _____

46 Calculate:

a 1.6 ÷ 0.4 _____

b 4.48 ÷ 0.8 _____

c 0.00715 ÷ 0.11 _____

d 144 ÷ 0.09 _____

47 Calculate, giving your answers correct to the number of decimal places indicated in brackets:

a 5.4 ÷ 0.7 (2) _____

b 12.8 ÷ 0.03 (3) _____

c 0.34 ÷ 3.6 (2) _____

d 0.66 ÷ 5.8 (3) _____

48 Find the value of:

a $\dfrac{6.4}{5 \times 0.2}$ _____

b $\dfrac{5.5 \times 0.6}{11}$ _____

c $\dfrac{7.2}{0.4 \times 0.6}$ _____

49 Express the following numbers as either all decimals or all fractions. Then write them in order of size, smallest first:

$\dfrac{7}{9}, \dfrac{4}{5}, \dfrac{9}{13}, 0.75$

_____

_____

50 Express as fractions in their lowest terms.

a 60% _____

b $10\frac{1}{2}$% _____

c 38% _____

d 96% _____

51 Express these percentages as decimals.

   a 56% _____

   b 12% _____

   c 140% _____

   d $28\frac{1}{2}$% _____

52 Express these decimals as percentages.

   a 1.74 _____

   b 0.56 _____

   c 0.35 _____

   d 0.04 _____

53 Deductions from Judy's pay were 20% for income tax and 12% for other deductions. What percentage did she keep?

_____

54 In a box of bananas 6% were bad. What percentage were good?

_____

55 Express the first quantity as a percentage of the second.

   a 40 cm, 100 cm _____

   b 150 cm², 25 cm² _____

   c 400 m, 2 km _____

   d 67.2 g, 80 g _____

56 Find the value of:

   a 66% of 325 m _____

   b 6% of 36 cm² _____

   c 12% of $48 600 _____

   d $2\frac{1}{3}$% of 270 m _____

57 Find the value of:

   a 8% of 1984 _____

   b 34% of $3500 _____

   c $33\frac{1}{3}$% 780 g _____

   d $5\frac{1}{8}$% of 400 kg _____

   e $66\frac{2}{3}$% of 231 cm² _____

   f $37\frac{1}{2}$% of 96 m _____

58 There are 160 houses in a street.
Thirty-five per cent of them have a pet.
How many houses:

   a have a pet _____

   b do not have a pet? _____

59 There are 60 shops in the High Street.
Thirty per cent of them sell food.
How many:

   a sell food _____

   b do not sell food? _____

60 During the course of a week, 360 patients attended Dr Khan's surgery.
Fifty-five per cent of these were males.

   a How many females attended his surgery?

_____

   b How many more males than females attended?

_____

61 In Year 7, 30% of the students take art, 20% take craft and 10% take both subjects. If there are 120 students in the year group, how many:

a take art

_____

b take craft

_____

c do not take either subject?

_____

62 At a school concert, 24% of the audience were boys, 36% were girls and the remainder were adults. If there were 250 people in the audience, how many adults attended?

_____

63 Last year, the amount I paid in rates on my property was \$72 000.

This year my rates have increased by $5\frac{1}{2}$%.

a How much is the increase?

_____

b How much are my rates this year?

_____

For the remaining questions, choose the letter that gives the correct answer.

64 To the nearest 100, 1549 is:

A 1500   **B** 1550

C 1600   **D** 1650

65 Written as a fraction, 2.6 is:

A $2\frac{4}{9}$ **B** $2\frac{6}{11}$

C $2\frac{3}{5}$ **D** $2\frac{4}{5}$

66 In the addition $53 + \square\,9 = 102$, the missing figure is:

A 1   **B** 3

C 4   **D** 5

67 Written as a decimal, $\frac{7}{10} + \frac{3}{1000}$ is:

A 0.73   **B** 0.703

C 0.0703   **D** 0.073

68 $0.4 \times 0.7 =$

A 0.0028   **B** 0.028

C 0.28   **D** 2.8

69 The HCF of 8, 16 and 28 is:

A 4   **B** 8

C 56   **D** 112

70 The prime numbers that are factors of 20 are:

A 2 and 4   **B** 2 and 10

C 2 and 5   **D** 4 and 5

71 The missing number in the subtraction $4.5\,\text{cm} - \square\,\text{mm} = 2.5\,\text{cm}$ is:

A 0.2   **B** 2

C 20   **D** 200

72 $0.4 \times 0.4 =$

A 0.000 16   **B** 0.0016

C 0.016   **D** 0.16

73 $0.5 \div 25 =$

A 0.002   **B** 0.02

C 0.2   **D** 2

74 $0.0034 \times 1000 =$

A 340   **B** 34

C 3.4   **D** 0.34

75 $2.22 - 0.3 - 1.02 =$

A 0.72   **B** 0.9

C 1.5   **D** 2.94

76 Expressed as a percentage $3\frac{3}{5}$ is:

A 40%   **B** 60%

C 340%   **D** 360%

77 72% expressed as a vulgar fraction in its lowest terms is:

A $\frac{12}{25}$ **B** $\frac{36}{50}$

C $\frac{18}{25}$ **D** $\frac{9}{14}$

78 Expressed as a percentage $\frac{7}{8}$ is:

A $72\frac{1}{2}$%   **B** 75%

C 80%   **D** $87\frac{1}{2}$%

79 84% of 3500 m is:

A 294 m   **B** 1680 m

C 2940 m   **D** 3290 m

80 Expressed as a percentage of 5.5 km, 1760 metres is:

A 30%   **B** 32%

C 36%   **D** 40%

81 Which one of the following statements is true?

A The next prime number after 29 is 37.

B The are six prime numbers between 4 and 20.

C There are exactly two prime numbers that are even numbers.

D The nearest prime number to 35 is 41.

82 Study the number 6 534 280. The digit that indicates the number of tens of thousands is:

A 2   **B** 3

C 5   **D** 6

83 The missing number in the subtraction 3.5 cm – ☐ mm = 2.4 cm is:

A 1.1   **B** 11

C 111   **D** 5.9

6 Measurement

1 Express the given quantity in terms of the unit in brackets:

   a 7 m (cm) _____

   b 12 km (m) _____

   c 24 cm (mm) _____

   d 56 km (cm) _____

   e 7.4 m (cm) _____

   f 6.2 m (mm) _____

   g 3.4 cm (mm) _____

   h 0.44 km (m) _____

2 Express the given quantity in terms of the unit in brackets:

   a 4 kg (g) _____

   b 15 t (kg) _____

   c 40 g (mg) _____

   d 3.5 t (kg) _____

   e 0.4 g (mg) _____

   f 1.8 kg (g) _____

   g 0.7 g (mg) _____

   h 0.8 kg (mg) _____

3 Express the given quantity in terms of the unit in brackets:

   a 1 m 40 cm (cm) _____

   b 5 cm 8 mm (mm) _____

   c 6 m 55 cm (cm) _____

   d 2 km 750 m (m) _____

   e 7 g 500 mg (mg) _____

   f 2 t 750 kg (kg) _____

   g 4 kg 200 g (g) _____

   h 1 kg 350 mg (mg) _____

4 Express the given quantity in terms of the unit in brackets:

   a 700 mm (cm) _____

   b 14 cm (m) _____

   c 3450 m (km) _____

   d 4 600 000 mm (km) _____

   e 650 g (kg) _____

   f 2200 mg (g) _____

   g 2500 kg (t) _____

   h 750 mg (g) _____

5 Express the given quantity in terms of the unit in brackets:

   a 2 m 75 cm (cm) _____

   b 7 km 40 m (km) _____

   c 6 cm 8 mm (cm) _____

   d 10 m 45 cm (m) _____

   e 3 kg 443 g (kg) _____

   f 7 kg 55 g (kg) _____

   g 4 kg 89 g (g) _____

   h 8 g 750 mg (mg) _____

6 Express the given quantity in terms of the unit in brackets:

   a 7 m + 56 cm (m) _____

   b 460 m + 3 km (km) _____

   c 6 cm + 8 mm (cm) _____

   d 550 mm + 46 cm + 2 m (m) _____

   e 2 m + 34 cm (mm) _____

   f 26 cm + 56 mm + 1 m (mm) _____

   g 2.8 km + 290 m (m) _____

   h 2 m + 39 cm + 600 mm (cm) _____

7 Express the sum or difference of the given quantities in terms of the unit in brackets:

   a   3t + 735 kg (kg)   ————————

   b   7 kg + 450 g (kg)   ————————

   c   44 kg + 0.3 t + 60 kg (kg) ————————

   d   2.8 t + 56 kg (kg)   ————————

   e   3 m − 78 cm (cm)   ————————

   f   2.4 m − 845 mm (cm)   ————————

   g   2.5 t − 774 kg (kg)   ————————

   h   4.6 kg − 845 g (g)   ————————

8 Calculate, giving your answer in the unit given in brackets:

   a   5 × 2 kg 420 g (g)   ————————

   b   7 × 3 m 44 cm (m)   ————————

   c   3 × 5 km 340 m (km)   ————————

9 Find, in metres, the perimeter of a rectangle in which the lengths of adjacent sides are 2.37 m and 560 cm.

————————————————————

10 Find the total mass, in kilograms, of 750 g of mixed fruit, 675 g of flour and 460 g of butter.

————————————————————

11 Express:

   a   5 dollars in cents   ————————

   b   16 dollars in cents   ————————

   c $1660 in cents.   ————————

12 Find the cost, in dollars, of 12 cans of cola at $75.50 a can.

————————————————————

13 Gas costs $185 a litre. How many complete litres can I buy for $5000?

————————————————————

14 Which is the better buy:

   i   75 g of coffee for $160

   ii   200 g for $370?

————————————————————

15 Express in mm³:

   a   12 cm³   ————————

   b   0.64 cm³   ————————

   c   0.06 cm³   ————————

   d   0.008 cm³   ————————

16 Express in cm³:

   a   5 m³   ————————

   b   0.73 m³   ————————

   c   420 mm³   ————————

   d   5750 mm³   ————————

17 Express in cm³:

   a   1.6 litres   ————————

   b   0.45 litres   ————————

   c   0.62 litres   ————————

   d   0.092 litres   ————————

18 Express in litres:

   a   6000 cm³   ————————

   b   36 000 cm³   ————————

   c   800 cm³   ————————

   d   470 000 cm³   ————————

19 Express in litres:

   a   3 m³   ————————

   b   2.4 m³   ————————

   c   0.082 m³   ————————

   d   0.66 m³   ————————

20 Express in litres:

    a $72\,000\,cm^3$ _____

    b $1.3\,m^3$ _____

    c $4\,545\,000\,cm^3$ _____

    d $0.052\,m^3$ _____

21 Express the given quantity in the unit(s) in brackets:

    a 8 yd 2 ft (ft)   _____

    b 3 ft 4 in (in)   _____

    c 1 mile 500 yd (yd)   _____

    d 5 ft 7 in (in)   _____

22 Express the given quantity in the unit(s) in brackets:

    a 3 yd 2 ft (ft)   _____

    b $1\frac{1}{2}$ miles (yd)   _____

    c 4 ft 5 in (in)   _____

    d 1 mile 450 ft (ft)   _____

23 Express the given quantity in the unit(s) in brackets:

    a 48 in (ft)   _____

    b 50 in (ft and in)   _____

    c 15 ft (yd)   _____

    d 70 ft (yd and ft)   _____

24 Express the given quantity in the unit(s) in brackets:

    a 3 lb 8 oz (oz)   _____

    b 2 tons 5 cwt (cwt)   _____

    c 63 oz (lb and oz)   _____

    d 160 lb (cwt and lb)   _____

25 Express the given quantity in the unit(s) in brackets:

    a 5 lb 2 oz (oz)   _____

    b 3 tons 10 cwt (cwt)   _____

    c 54 oz (lb and oz)   _____

    d 240 lb (cwt and lb)   _____

26 Write the first quantity roughly in terms of the unit in brackets:

    a 4 kg (lb)   _____

    b 10 lb (kg)   _____

    c 50 miles (kilometres)   _____

    d 200 km (miles)   _____

27 Write the first quantity roughly in terms of the unit in brackets:

    a 5 kg (lb)   _____

    b 100 miles (kilometres)   _____

    c 300 km (miles)   _____

    d 22 lb (kg)   _____

28 Which is heavier:

    a a 6 lb of carrots or a 4 kg bag of carrots

    _____

    b a 20 kg bag of cement or a 56 lb bag of cement?

    _____

29 Which is the larger page size:

    i 240 mm × 165 mm   **ii** 10 in × 7 in?

    _____

30 The instructions for repotting a plant say that it should go in a 20 cm pot. The flower pots I have are marked 5 in, 8 in and 10 in. Which one should I use?

    _____

31 Which rectangle has the smaller area:

   i one measuring 300 mm by 200 mm

   ii one measuring 12 in by 8 in?

_____

32

21 ft

33 ft

What are the approximate dimensions of this rectangle in metres?

_____

33 Nabez went to watch a cricket match. As soon as the match finished he went home. He took 13 minutes to walk to the bus stop, where he waited for 7 minutes before the bus arrived. The bus ride took 35 minutes and he had a 12 minute walk before he reached home at 19.33. What time did the match finish?

_____

34 Here is John's schedule for today.

7.10	Get up
7.25	Leave home
7.55	Arrive at work (5 minutes early)
10.20 – 10.30	Morning break
12.30 – 1.00	Lunch break
2.50 – 3.00	Afternoon break
5.00	Finish work
5.35	Arrive home
6.30 – 7.00	Main meal
8.30	Go out
11.30	Return home
11.45	Go to bed

a How long is it from the time John gets up until he is due to start work? _____

b How long is it from the time he gets up until he goes to bed? _____

c How long is he at home after work before he goes out? _____

d What is the length of his working day:

   i including breaks _____

   ii excluding breaks? _____

e How much longer does he work in the morning than in the afternoon?

_____

f How much sleep does he normally get from one working day to the next?

_____

35 To convert from degrees Fahrenheit to degrees Celsius, the rule is 'subtract 32, multiply your answer by 5, then divide by 9'. Convert:

a 212 °F to °C   _____

b 32 °F to °C   _____

c 50 °F to °C   _____

36 To convert from degrees Celsius to degrees Fahrenheit the rule is: multiply by 9, divide your answer by 5 then add 32. Convert:

a 100 °C to °F

_____

b 0 °C to °F

_____

c 60 °C to °F

_____

37 Write down the unit that would be the most sensible to measure:

a the mass of a tablet of soap _____

b the length of a truck _____

c the distance between Trinidad and Barbados _____

d the time it takes to fly in a jet from Kingston to New York. _____

38 A field has four sides. The lengths of three of the sides are 58 m, 136 m and 205 m. If the perimeter of the field is 536 m, find the length of the fourth side.

_____

39 Use these instructions to convert –6 °C to degrees Fahrenheit:

i Multiply –6 by 9 _____

ii Divide your answer by 5 _____

iii Add 32 to your answer. _____

40 Express the given quantities in terms of the unit in brackets:

a 0.06 m (mm) _____

b 2.4 t (kg) _____

c 3 g (mg) _____

d 3.5 kg (g) _____

41 Express the given quantities in terms of the unit in brackets:

a 6 km 500 m (km) _____

b 750 mg (g) _____

c 850 g (kg) _____

d 30 cm³ (m³) _____

42 Express the given quantities in terms of the unit in brackets

a 7 t (kg) _____

b 6 hours (minutes) _____

c 5 g (mg) _____

d 1000 days (years and days) _____

For questions **43** to **56**, choose the letter that gives the correct answer.

43 3.4 cm is equal to:

A 0.34 mm   **B** 34 mm

C 340 mm   **D** 3400 mm

44 7.3 cm is equal to:

A 0.0073 m   **B** 0.73 m

C 73 mm   **D** 730 mm

45 Expressed in grams, 8 kilograms is:

A 80 g   **B** 800 g

C 8000 g   **D** 80 000 g

46 Expressed in tonnes, 65 000 kg is:

A 0.65 t   **B** 6.5 t

C 65 t   **D** 650 t

47 4 yd 2 ft is equal to:

A 12 ft   **B** 14 ft

C 16 ft   **D** 18 ft

48 54 inches is equal to:

A 3 ft 4 in   **B** 4 ft 8 in

C 4 ft 6 in   **D** 4 ft 4 in

49 Expressed in years and days, 740 days is:

A 2 years   **B** 2 yr 10 days

C 2 yr 15 days   **D** 2 yr 20 days

50 The dates of birth of four children are 9-10-11, 20-4-12, 16-8-11, 19-3-11. The youngest was born on:

A 19-3-11   **B** 20-4-12

B 9-10-11   **D** 16-8-11

51 The period of time from 0740 hours and 1430 hours is:

A 6h 40min   **B** 6h 50min

C 7h 10min   **D** 7h 40min

52 The number of minutes from 10.32 am to 1.15 pm the same day is:

A 103   **B** 123

C 133   **D** 163

53 The number of pounds in 2 cwt 40 lb is:

A 152   **B** 240

C 244   **D** 264

54 My grandfather was born on 8 December 1936 and died on 10 June 2019. How old was he when he died?

A 81   **B** 82

C 83   **D** 84

55 Simon was born on 28 December 1999. How old will he be on Christmas Day 2050?

A 50   **B** 51

C 52   **D** 53

56 Hettie will be 50 on 7 May 2040. In what year was she born?

A 1988   **B** 1989

C 1990   **D** 1991

7 Area and perimeter

1 These shapes are drawn on 5 mm squared paper (not to scale). Find the perimeter of each shape.

a   **b**

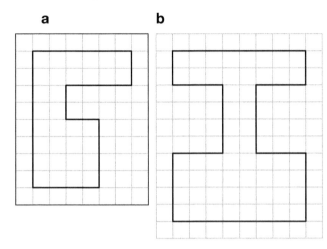

_____ _____

2 First estimate, and then find accurately, the perimeter of each shape.

a

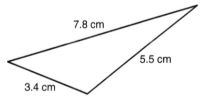

7.8 cm

5.5 cm

3.4 cm

_____ _____

b

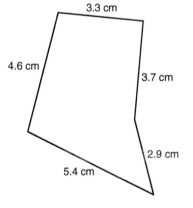

3.3 cm

4.6 cm

3.7 cm

2.9 cm

5.4 cm

_____ _____

c

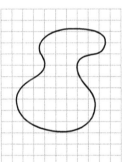

35 mm

33 mm   37 mm

62 mm

_____ _____

In questions **3** to **10**, count squares to estimate the area of each shape.

3   **4**

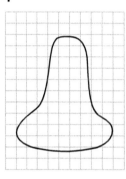

_____ _____

5   **6**

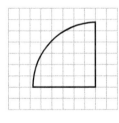
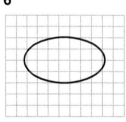

_____ _____

7   **8**

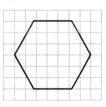
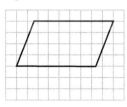

_____ _____

47

9

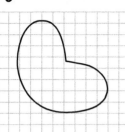

10

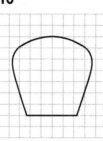

_____   _____

Find the area of each of the following shapes, clearly stating the units of your answer.

11 A square of side 7 cm

_____

12 A square of side 2.6 m

_____

13 A rectangle measuring 9 cm by 12 cm

_____

14 A rectangle with adjacent sides 3.6 cm and 4.8 cm

_____

15 A square of side 56 km

_____

16 A rectangle measuring 1.7 m by 2.6 m

_____

17 A square of side 0.45 m

_____

18 A rectangle measuring 50 mm by 34 mm

_____

Find the area of the rectangles in questions **19** to **22**.

Give your answer in the unit in brackets.

19 A rectangle measuring 55 mm by 7 cm. (cm^2)

_____

20 A rectangle measuring 45 mm by 6 cm. (mm^2)

_____

21 A rectangle measuring 34 mm by 4.5 cm. (cm^2)

_____

22 A rectangle measuring 450 cm by 7 m. (m^2)

_____

In questions **23** to **30**, each shape is made from rectangles. For each shape find:

a its perimeter

b its area.

All measurements are in centimetres.

23

a _____

b _____

24

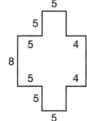

a _____

b _____

25

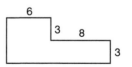

a _____

b _____

26

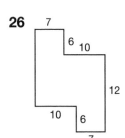

a _____

b _____

27

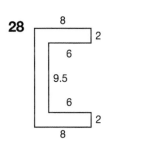

a _____

b _____

28

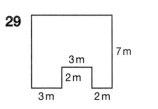

a _____

b _____

29

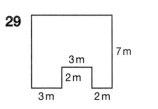

a _____

b _____

30

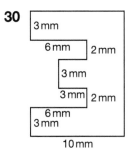

a _____

b _____

In questions **31** to **33**, find the area that is shaded.

All measurements are in centimetres.

31

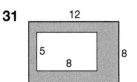

_____

32

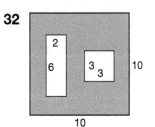

_____

33

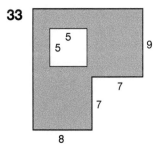

_____

34 Sketch a square of side 6 cm. How many squares of side 2 cm are needed to cover it?

_____

35 A square has a side of length 12 cm. How many squares of side 3 cm are needed to cover it?

_____

36 A rectangle measures 8 cm by 6 cm. How many squares of side 2 cm are needed to cover it?

_____

37 The side of a square is 20 cm. How many squares of side 4 cm are needed to cover it?

_____

38 How many squares of side 4 cm are needed to cover a rectangle measuring 20 cm by 24 cm?

_____

39 How many squares of side 6 cm are needed to cover a rectangle measuring 42 cm by 36 cm?

_____

40 Express in cm^2:

  a $0.07 m^2$ _____

  b $0.55 m^2$ _____

  c $6\frac{1}{2} m^2$ _____

41 Express in mm^2:

  a $8 m^2$ _____

  b $5500 cm^2$ _____

42 Express in m^2:

  a $7500 cm^2$ _____

  b $450\,000 cm^2$ _____

43 Express in km^2:

  a $890\,000 m^2$ _____

  b $23\,000\,000 cm^2$ _____

44 Express in cm^2:

  a $60 mm^2$ _____

  b $0.035 m^2$ _____

  c $95\,000 mm^2$ _____

In questions **45** to **52**, find the area of each of the rectangles, giving your answer in the unit given:

	Length	Breadth	
45	5 m	0.3 m	cm^2
46	70 mm	4.5 cm	mm^2
47	0.8 m	0.6 m	cm^2
48	800 cm	500 cm	m^2
49	$2\frac{1}{2}$ m	$\frac{1}{2}$ m	cm^2
50	3.5 cm	2.4 cm	mm^2
51	340 m	250 m	km^2
52	56 cm	65 mm	cm^2

In questions **53** to **56**, find:

  a the area of the surface

  b the perimeter of the surface.

53 A square board for playing draughts or chess with side 32 cm.

  a _____

  b _____

54 A hockey pitch measuring 57 m by 91 m.

  a _____

  b _____

55 A football pitch measuring 110 yd by 60 yd.

   a _____

   b _____

56 A pool table measuring 1.83 m by 3.66 m.

   a _____

   b _____

57 A roll of paper is 22 cm wide and 5 m long.

Find:

   a its area in cm^2

    _____

   b its perimeter when unrolled, in cm

    _____

   c its area in m^2.

    _____

58 How many square tiles, of side 20 cm are needed to cover a wall measuring 3.8 m by 2.4 m?

    _____

59 My rectangular bathroom measures 2.1 m by 1.95 m. The rectangular area covered by the bath measures 190 cm by 75 cm and the pedestal for the hand basin covers $200 cm^2$.

Work out:

   a the perimeter of the bathroom, in m

    _____

   b the floor area of the bathroom, in m^2

    _____

   c the area of floor-covering needed, in m^2.

    _____

60 Clive wants to tile a wall 4.2 m wide and 2.4 m high with tiles measuring 15 cm by 20 cm. He would like the longer side of each tile to be vertical.

   a Can he do this without cutting any tiles?

    _____

   b How many tiles measuring 15 cm by 20 cm are needed to tile this wall if no tile is cut?

    _____

   c The tiles are sold in boxes, each holding 100 tiles. How many boxes must he buy?

    _____

61 Jenny's lounge is rectangular and measures 5.5 m by 4.5 m. She lays a rectangular carpet, measuring 4 m by 3.5 m in the centre of the room. If the carpet costs $3850 per square metre, find:

   a the cost of the carpet

    _____

   b the area of Jenny's lounge that is not covered by the carpet.

    _____

62 A cricket pitch is 66 feet long and 12 feet wide. The distance between the batting creases is 58 feet.

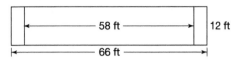

Find:

a the area of the pitch in:

   i square feet

_____

   ii square yards.

_____

b the area between the batting creases.

_____

c the perimeter of the pitch in:

   i feet

_____

   ii yards.

_____

1 Name these basic shapes.

a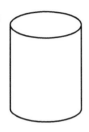

_____

b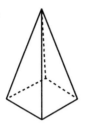

_____

c

_____

d

_____

e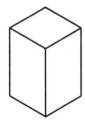

_____

f

_____

2 Name the basic shapes used to make each of these solids:

a

_____

b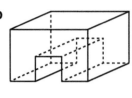

_____

c

_____

d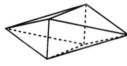

_____

e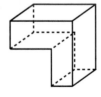

_____

_____

f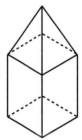

_____

_____

3 This net, which is drawn to scale on squared paper, will make a cuboid.

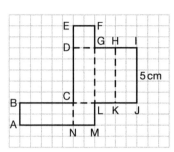

a Sketch the cuboid, and show its measurements.

b How many faces does it have?

_____

c What shape describes the ends of this cuboid?

_____

d Work out the perimeter of the net.

_____

e Work out the total surface area of the cuboid.

_____

f Which corners meet at A?

_____

g Which corners meet at H?

_____

4 Which unit would you use to give the volume of:

a a train _____

b a mobile phone _____

c an eraser _____

d a waste-paper bin _____

e an apple _____

f a bead? _____

5

a How many edges does this cube have?

_____

b How many faces does it have?

_____

c What is the area of one face?

_____

d What is the total surface area of the cube?

_____

Two identical cubes are stuck together.

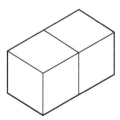

e What name do we give to this shape?

_____

f For this shape, give the number of:

  i edges _____

  ii surfaces. _____

6 A rectangular piece of card measures 11 cm by 9 cm. Four squares with sides of 3 cm are cut from the corners to give the net for an open box.

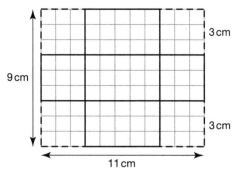

a What are the measurements of the box?

_____

b What is the area of the original piece of card?

_____

c What area is removed?

_____

d What area remains to form the net for this open box?

_____

7 The diagram shows part of the net of an open rectangular box measuring 6 cm by 3 cm by 2 cm.

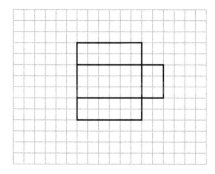

a Complete the net by showing the three possible positions where you can place the missing side. Mark them A, B and C.

b Calculate the area of card used to make the box.

_____

8 The diagram shows part of the net for a cuboid measuring 4 cm by 3 cm by 2 cm.

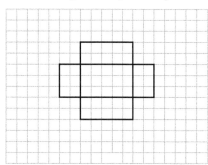

a Complete the net showing the four possible positions for the missing side. Mark them A, B, C and D.

b Work out the area of card used to make the cuboid.

_____

9 The diagram shows a pyramid with a square base. All the edges of this solid are of length 6 cm.

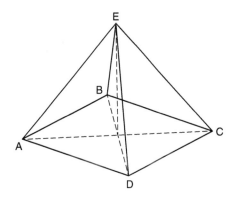

a Sketch a net for this solid. Label it and insert the measurements.

10 This net will make a cuboid.

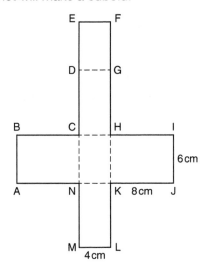

a Sketch the cuboid and show its measurements.

b How many triangles are exactly the same size as triangle CDE? Name them.

_____

c Find the total distance:

   i around the base ABCD

   _____

   ii around triangle ABE.

   _____

d How many edges does this solid have?

_____

e What is the sum of the lengths of all these edges?

_____

b Which edge joins with:

   i BC   _____

   ii ML   _____

   iii GH?   _____

c Which corners meet at:

   i M   _____

   ii I   _____

   iii B?   _____

d How many edges of this cuboid are of length 8 cm?

_____

In questions **1–4**, measure the angles shown.

1

2

3

4

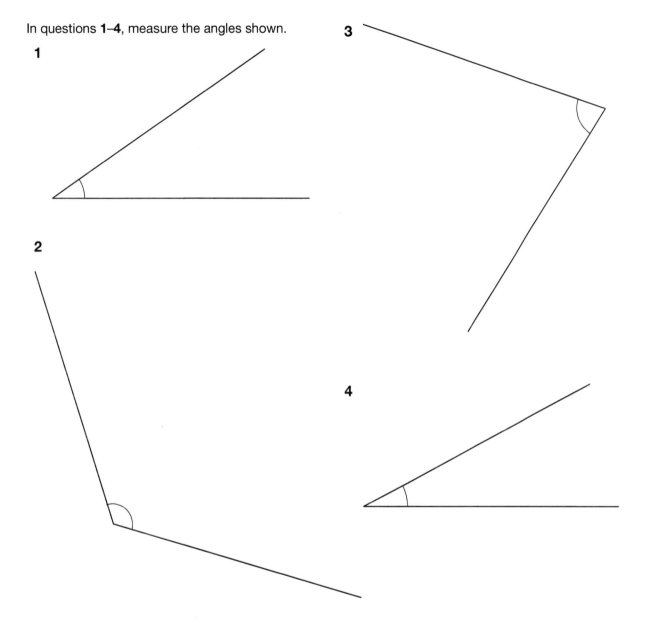

5 Use your protractor to draw the following angles accurately:

a 37°

b 170°

c 52°

d 120°

e 135°

6 a Draw any angle PQR similar to the one shown below.

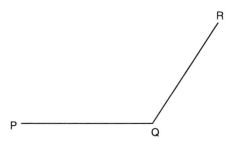

b Construct the line through R parallel to PQ.

c Construct the line through P parallel to QR to cross the line through R at S.

d Measure the lengths of PQ and RS. How do they compare?

_____

e Measure the lengths of PS and QR. How do they compare?

_____

7 a Draw any triangle ABC, similar to the one shown below.

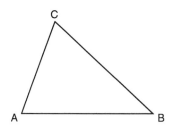

8 a Draw any angle ABC similar to the one shown below.

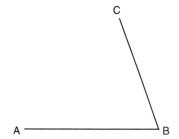

b Construct the perpendicular from C to AB to meet AB at D.

c Construct the perpendicular from A to BC to meet BC at E.

d Construct the perpendicular from B to AC to meet AC at F.

e What do you notice about the three lines AE, CD and BF?

b Construct the perpendicular bisectors of AB and BC.

c Mark the point where the bisectors intersect X.

d Draw a circle with centre X and radius XA. Does this circle pass through the points B and C?

In questions **1** to **7** draw the image of each object in the mirror line.

1

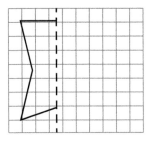

2

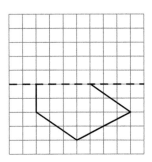

3

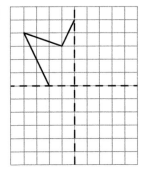

4

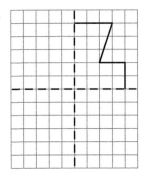

5

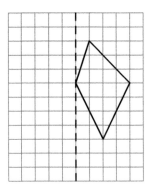

6

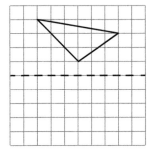

7

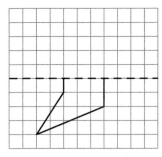

In questions **8** to **10**, draw the image of the given object. The vertices of the object are labelled A,B,C, etc. Label the corresponding vertices of the images A′, B′, C′, etc.

8

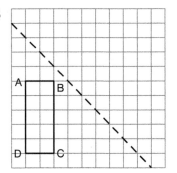

9

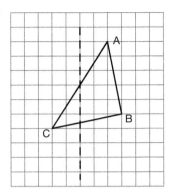

10

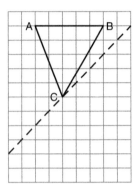

11 Draw the images of the given shapes in the mirror line.

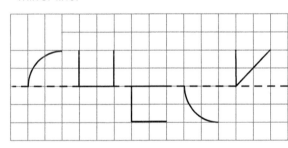

What word is now spelt?

_____

In questions **12** to **16**, draw the mirror line.

12

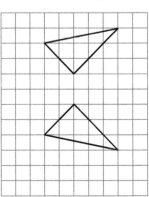

13

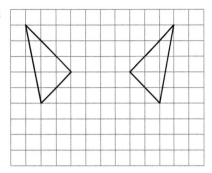

14

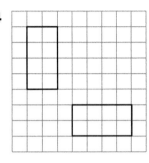

15

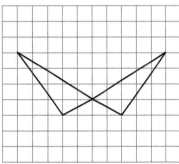

16

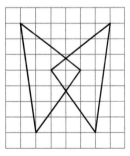

17 Draw △ABC where the vertices are the points (2, 6), B(7, 8), C(8, 4) and △A'B'C' where the vertices are the points A'(2, 2), B'(7, 0), C'(8, 4).

Draw the mirror line so that △A'B'C' is the reflection of △ABC.

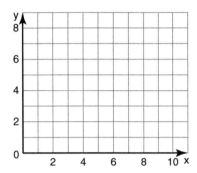

Are there any invariant points? If so name them.

18 In this diagram, which images of △ABC are given by reflections?

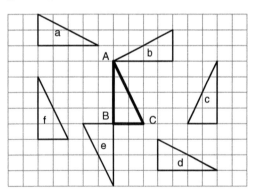

19 Use this shape to make a strip pattern using:

a reflections in a line outside the shape

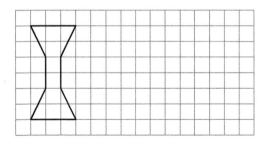

b reflections in a line through the shape.

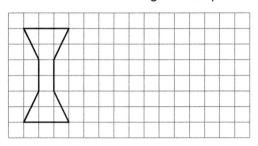

In questions **20** and **21**, describe the translation that translates the shape with solid lines to give the shape with dotted lines.

20

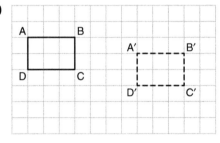

21

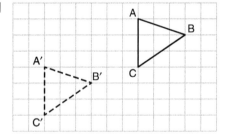

In questions **22** and **23**, translate the given shape according to the instruction.

22

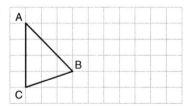

7 squares to the right

1 square down

23

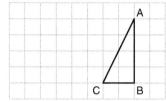

6 squares to the left

1 square up

Each of the diagrams in questions **24** to **26** has rotational symmetry of the order given.

If X marks the centre of rotation complete the diagram.

24 Rotational symmetry of order 4

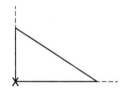

25 Rotational symmetry of order 3

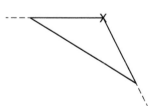

26 Rotational symmetry of order 2

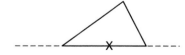

In questions **27** to **32**, which of the following shapes have:

    a rotational symmetry only

    b line symmetry only

    c both?

27 _____

28 _____

29 _____

30 _____

31 _____

32 _____

In questions **33** and **34**, mark the centre of rotation with a cross and also the angle of rotation.

33

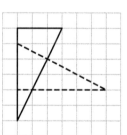

34

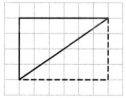

In questions **35** to **37**, draw the images of the given objects under the rotations described.

The centre of rotation is marked with a cross.

35 Angle of rotation 180°

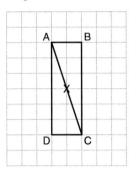

36 Angle of rotation 90° anticlockwise

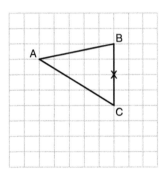

37 Angle of rotation 90° clockwise

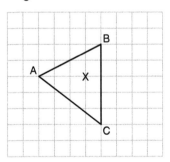

In questions **38** to **41**, mark the centre of rotation with a cross and give the angle of rotation.

38

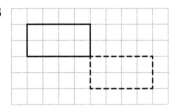

39

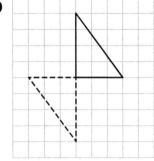

40

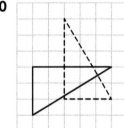

41

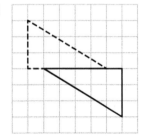

In questions **1** to **12**, choose the letter that gives the correct answer.

1 Expressed in metres, 0.06 km is:

A 6 m   **B** 60 m

C 600 m   **D** 6000 m

2 Expressed in cm, 520 mm is:

A 0.0052 cm   **B** 0.052 cm

C 0.52 cm   **D** 52 cm

3 Expressed in km, 750 m is:

A 0.075 km   **B** 0.75 km

C 7.5 km   **D** 75 km

4 Expressed in mm, 24.6 cm is:

A 2.46 mm   **B** 24.6 mm

C 246 mm   **D** 2460 mm

5 Expressed in grams, 0.45 kg is:

A 45 000 g   **B** 4500 g

C 450 g   **D** 45 g

6 Expressed in kg, 8450 g is:

A 0.845 kg   **B** 8.45 kg

C 84.5 kg   **D** 845 kg

7 Expressed in litres, 18 000 cm^3 is:

A 1800 litres   **B** 180 litres

C 18 litres   **D** 1.8 litres

8 Expressed in cm^3, 4.5 litres is:

A 0.45 cm^3 **B** 45 cm^3

C 450 cm^3 **D** 4500 cm^3

9 Expressed in yards, 39 ft is:

A 13 yd   **B** 14 yd

C 15 yd   **D** 16 yd

10 Expressed in ft and in, 65 in is:

A 5 ft 5 in   **B** 5 ft 9 in

C 6 ft 3 in   **D** 6 ft 5 in

11 Expressed in kg, 25 lb is roughly:

A 5 kg   **B** 8 kg

C 10 kg   **D** 11 kg

12 Expressed in lb and oz, 30 oz is:

A 1 lb 4 oz   **B** 1 lb 8 oz

C 1 lb 14 oz   **D** 2 lb 2 oz

13 Express:

a 3500 m in kilometres

_____

b 540 mm in centimetres

_____

c 4250 g in kilograms

_____

d 84.3 cm in millimetres

_____

14 Express:

a 106 inches in feet and inches

_____

b 34 ft in yards and feet

_____

c $2\frac{1}{2}$ miles in yards

_____

d 6000 yd in miles and yards

_____

15 Express:

a 2 lb 6 oz in ounces

_____

b 65 oz in lb and oz

_____

c 34 000 cm³ in litres

_____

d 5.8 litres in cm³

_____

16 Amanda went shopping. She walked 5 minutes to the bus stop, and waited 8 minutes before the bus arrived. The bus took 12 minutes to get to the shopping centre where Amanda got off. She spent 1 hour and 35 minutes at the shopping centre before waiting at the bus stop for the return trip home. The bus arrived in 3 minutes and took exactly the same time to take her to the bus stop near her home as it had for her to ride in. It took a further 9 minutes before she was back at home.

a How long was it from the time she left home until she returned?

_____

b If she arrived home at 1.48 pm what time had she left in the morning?

_____

In questions **17** to **19**, find the area of each shape, clearly stating the units of each answer.

17 A square of side 4.4 cm.

_____

18 A rectangle measuring 46 cm by 8 cm.

_____

19 A rectangle with adjacent sides 4.2 cm and 5.5 cm.

_____

In questions **20** to **24**, find the area of each rectangle, giving your answer in the unit in brackets.

	Length	Breadth	
20	36 cm	8.5 mm	(cm²)
21	$3\frac{1}{2}$ m	$\frac{1}{2}$ m	(cm²)
22	50 mm	2.5 cm	(mm²)
23	120 cm	40 cm	(m²)
24	20 mm	1.5 cm	(cm²)

25 The area of a square is 36 cm². Find:

a the length of a side

_____

b its perimeter.

_____

26 The area of a rectangle is 40 cm². The length of the longer sides is 8 cm. Find:

a the length of a shorter side

_____

b its perimeter.

_____

27 The perimeter of a rectangle is 34 cm. The length of the longer sides is 9 cm. Find:

a the length of one of the shorter sides

_____

b its area.

_____

28 A rectangular table top measures 90 cm by 65 cm. Find:

   a its perimeter in metres ————————

   b its area in square metres. ————————

29 A rectangular games field measures 550 m by 280 m. Find:

   a its perimeter in metres ————————

   b its area in square metres. ————————

30 The area of a rectangle is 480 cm². One side is of length 24 cm. Find:

   a its dimensions ————————

   b its perimeter. ————————

In questions **31** to **34**, each shape is made from rectangles. Clearly stating the units of your answer, find:

a its perimeter

b its area

All measurements are given in centimetres.

31

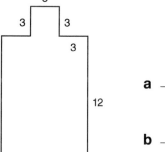

   a ————————

   b ————————

32

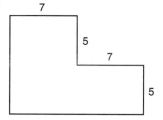

   a ————————————————

   b ————————————————

33

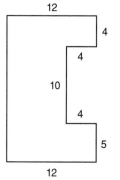

   a ————————————————

   b ————————————————

34

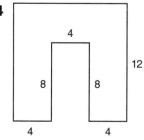

   a ————————————————

   b ————————————————

In questions **35** and **36**, find the area that is shaded. All dimensions are in centimetres.

35

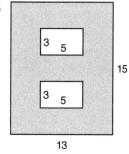

36

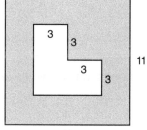

67

37 This net will make a cuboid.
All dimensions are in centimetres.

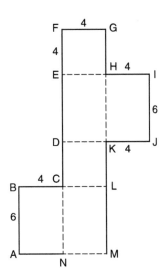

a Sketch the cuboid alongside the net and show its measurements.

b Which edge joins with:

   i BC   _____

   ii IJ   _____

   iii HI?   _____

c Which corners meet at:

   i I   _____

   ii B   _____

   iii F?   _____

d How many edges of this cuboid are of length 6 cm?

_____

e How many faces does the cuboid have?

_____

f Find the perimeter of the given net.

_____

g Is it possible to draw a different net that will make the same cuboid but has a shorter perimeter?

If your answer is 'yes' sketch the net.

_____

38 Consider the angles 145°, 65°, 47°, 90°, 127°, 56°, 256°. Which of these angles are:

a acute _____

b obtuse _____

c neither. _____

In questions **39** to **41**, describe the translation that translates the solid shape to the shape with the dotted outline.

39

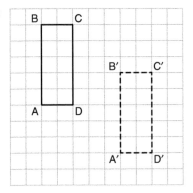

40

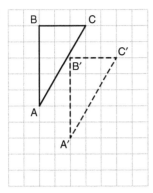

41

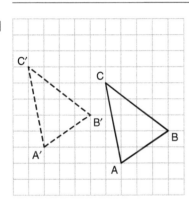

In questions **42** and **43**, translate the given shape according to the instructions.

42

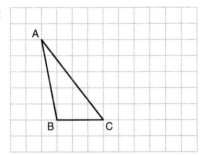

6 squares to the right
2 squares up

43

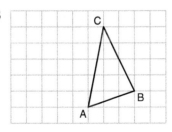

5 squares to the left
1 square up

44 Complete the diagram so that the resulting shape has rotational symmetry of order 4 about the cross.

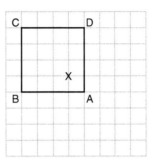

In questions **45** and **46**, mark the centre of rotation with a cross and give the angle of rotation.

45

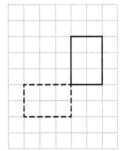

46

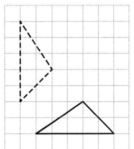

47

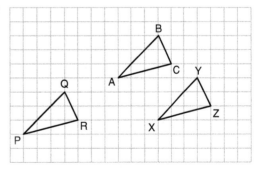

Give the displacements right/left, and up/down describing the translation that maps:

a △ABC to △XYZ

b △ABC to △PQR

_____

c △PQR to △XYZ

_____

d △XYZ to △ABC

_____

48

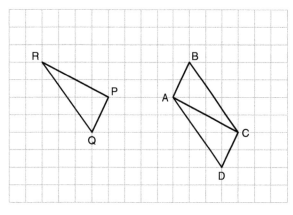

a Give the angle of rotation and the centre of rotation when:

   i △ABC is mapped to △PQR

   _____

   ii △ABC is mapped to △CDA

   _____

b Describe the transformation that maps △PQR to △CDA.

_____

In questions **49** and **50** draw the mirror line.

49

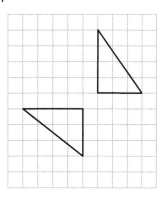

50

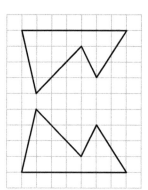

51

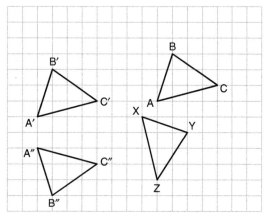

Describe the transformation that maps:

a △ABC to △XYZ

_____

b △ABC to △A'B'C'

_____

c △A'B'C' to △A"B"C"

_____

For a translation, give the displacement right/left and up/down to get to the new position.

For a reflection, draw the mirror line.

For a rotation, draw the centre of rotation and the angle of rotation.

11 Ratio and proportion

1 Give the following ratios in their simplest form:

  a 24 : 16   _____

  b 64 : 72   _____

  c $\frac{1}{6} : \frac{2}{3} : \frac{1}{2}$ _____

  d 81 : 54 : 135   _____

  e $3\frac{2}{3} : 5\frac{1}{2}$ _____

2 Which is the larger ratio?

  a 20 : 7 or 23 : 8   _____

  b 3 : 11 or 5 : 22   _____

3 Simplify the following ratios:

  a 53c : $1.59   _____

  b 35 cm : 0.2 m   _____

  c 675 mg : 1 g   _____

4 Find the ratio of the following prices:

  a $84 for 12 to $8 each

    _____

  b $50 per kg to $40 000 per tonne

    _____

  c $2700 per metre to $36 per cm.

    _____

5 Simplify the ratios:

  a 20 : 12   _____

  b $3 : 75c   _____

  c 133 : 171   _____

6 Simplify the ratios:

  a 10 : 15 : 30   _____

  b 9 : 45 : 63   _____

  c 84 : 35 : 21   _____

7 Express the following ratios in their simplest form:

  a $3 : \frac{1}{3}$ _____

  b $4 : \frac{2}{5}$ _____

  c $\frac{1}{5} : \frac{1}{6}$ _____

8 Which is the smaller ratio?

  a 7 : 5 or 3 : 2   _____

  b 13 : 7 or 7 : 4   _____

9 Which is the larger ratio?

  a 4 : 7 or 5 : 9   _____

  b 8 : 9 or 10 : 11   _____

    _____

10 Identify the equivalent ratios in each set.

  a 25 : 35, 30 : 45, 5 : 7   _____

  b $\frac{5}{8} : \frac{7}{8}, \frac{5}{4} : \frac{4}{3}$, 15 : 16   _____

11 The ratio of the number of girls to the number of boys in a class is 7 : 5. There are 15 boys. How many girls are there?

    _____

12 **a** Divide $56 into two parts in the ratio 5 : 2.

    _____

  b Divide 135 m into three parts in the ratio 1 : 3 : 5.

    _____

  c Divide 1 hour 17 minutes into three parts in the ratio 2 : 3 : 6.

    _____

13 a Divide a rod of length 144 cm into two parts in the ratio 7 : 5.

_____

b Divide $43 200 into three parts in the ratio 3 : 4 : 5.

_____

c Divide 646 kg into three parts in the ratio 4 : 6 : 9.

_____

14 A sum of money is divided into two parts in the ratio 3 : 5. The larger amount is $750 more than the smaller amount. How much money is divided into two parts?

_____

15 Find the missing numbers in the following ratios:

a $3 : 5 = 6 :$ ___   **b** $\dfrac{}{6} : \dfrac{8}{12}$

c $5 :$ ___ $= 40 : 48$

16 Two lengths are in the ratio 7 : 9. The second length is 81 cm. What is the first length?

_____

17 The length, originally 8 cm, is increased so that the ratio of the new length to the old length is 5 : 4. What is the new length?

_____

18 The ratio of the length of a model airplane to the length of the actual airplane is 1 : 450. The model is 10 cm long. How long is the actual airplane?

_____

19 Divide $18 000 into two parts in the ratio 5 : 4.

_____

20 Sandy is 12 years old and Elsie is 14 years old. Divide £3120 between them in the ratio of their ages. Would your answer be the same if they were each one year older?

_____

21 Divide $20 000 into two parts in the ratio 1 : 9.

_____

22 In a bowl containing oranges and pears, the ratio of the number of oranges to the number of pears is 5 : 3. If there are 32 pieces of fruit altogether how many pears are there?

_____

23 A length of rope is cut into two pieces. The longer piece is 60% of the original piece. What is the ratio of the lengths of the two pieces?

_____

24 A sum of money is divided between Morgan and Joe in the ratio 9 : 7. Morgan receives $22 140. How much does Joe receive?

_____

25 Divide $68 000 amongst three people so that their shares are in the ratio 5 : 6 : 5.

_____

26 Find the map ratio of the map in which:

a 4 cm on the map represents 1 km

_____

b 10 km is represented by 5 cm on the map

_____

c $\frac{1}{2}$ cm on the map represents 1500 m

_____

d 1 km is represented by 10 cm on the map.

_____

27 The map ratio of a map is 1 : 20 000. The distance between Amberley and Bexeter on the map is 10 cm. What is the true distance between Amberley and Bexeter?

_____

28 The map ratio of a map is 1 : 2 000 000. Find the distance on the map which represents an actual distance of 45 km.

_____

29 One litre of fuel takes a car 22 km. At the same rate how far does this car travel on:

a 4 litres _____

b 5.6 litres? _____

30 The cost of 1 kg of mixed vegetables is $264. Find the cost of 34 kg.

_____

31 Six cups and saucers cost $1920. What is the cost of one cup and saucer?

_____

32 The cost of running an electric fan for 4.5 hours is $23.40. What is the cost of running the fan for 1 hour?

_____

33 A machine uses 6 units of electricity in 4 hours. How many units does it use in 5 hours?

_____

34 A machine consumes 8 units of electricity in 6 hours.

a How many units would in consume in:

i 12 hours

_____

ii 9 hours?

_____

b How many hours would the machine run on:

i 24 units

_____

ii 20 units?

_____

35 A $\frac{1}{2}$ kg bag of sweets cost $600. At the same rate what would a $1\frac{3}{4}$ kg bag cost?

_____

36 Pamela changed EC$55 into US dollars and got $25 for them. How many US dollars would she get for EC$616?

_____

37 It cost $132 000 for tickets for a group of 12 students to attend a concert. How much would it cost for tickets for 19 students?

_____

38 An 8 kg bag of potatoes cost $336. At the same rate, what would a 50 kg bag cost?

_____

39 A school allows 95 exercise books a year for every five students. How many exercise books are needed for 24 students for a year?

_____

40 A recipe for Chinese bean sprouts to serve four lists the following ingredients:

50 g chicken   20 ml peanut oil

4 spring onions   500 g bean sprouts

root ginger   80 ml chicken stock

4 celery sticks   10 ml soy sauce

100 g mushrooms

a What will be the cost of the peanut oil used, if it is sold in litre bottles at $200 each?

_____

b Chicken costs $224 per kg. How much will the chicken cost?

_____

c A bottle of soy sauce contains 150 ml. How many servings of Chinese bean sprouts should this bottle be sufficient for?

_____

d List the ingredients to serve 10 people.

_____

_____

_____

_____

_____

41 A recipe for a fruit cake includes the following ingredients:

175 g currants   125 g sultanas

50 g raisins   40 g glacé cherries

40 g almonds   125 g plain flour

75 g margarine   90 g soft brown sugar

2 eggs

For a smaller cake, these ingredients are needed in the same proportions.

For a cake that uses 100 g of plain flour, how much of each of the following ingredients will be needed?

currants

_____

raisins

_____

soft brown sugar

_____

glacé cherries

_____

margarine

_____

42 A recipe for cream of mushroom soup to serve four people includes the following ingredients:

25 g plain flour

25 g margarine

275 ml chicken stock

275 ml milk

100 g chopped mushrooms

Estimate the amount of each of these ingredients that will be required to make enough soup for 10 servings. Round each mass correct to the nearest 5 g and each amount of fluid correct to the nearest 5 ml.

plain flour

margarine

chicken stock

milk

chopped mushrooms

43 Kevin buys enough turf to lay a rectangular lawn measuring 36 m by 24 m. Before laying the turf he changes his mind. He decides that his rectangular lawn will be 32 m long. If he lays all the turf how wide is it?

44 A short story is 121 lines with an average of 15 words per line. It is retyped with an average of 11 words per line. How many lines will there be?

45 A spreadsheet containing the results of a survey has 34 rows with 12 cells in each row. The same results can be entered in the same total number of cells but with 24 rows. How many cells are needed in each row?

46 In a factory, 63 machines are needed to produce the required number of units in 48 hours. How many machines are needed to produce the same number of units in 42 hours?

47 In a large company, 30 offices are needed if the staff are accommodated 8 to an office. How many offices would be needed if they are rearranged to accommodate 10 to an office?

48 A book is 156 pages long if the text is arranged with 39 lines to each page. How many pages will be required if the text is reset with the same size type but with 36 lines to a page?

12 Statistics

1 The shoe sizes of a group of boys were recorded as:

6 10 $6\frac{1}{2}$ 9 $6\frac{1}{2}$ 6 8 $6\frac{1}{2}$ 10 10 $7\frac{1}{2}$ $9\frac{1}{2}$

$6\frac{1}{2}$ 7 7 $10\frac{1}{2}$ $7\frac{1}{2}$ 7 $8\frac{1}{2}$ $8\frac{1}{2}$ 9 $7\frac{1}{2}$ $9\frac{1}{2}$ $7\frac{1}{2}$

7 11 7 7 $8\frac{1}{2}$ 9 $8\frac{1}{2}$ $6\frac{1}{2}$ 6 8 8 $8\frac{1}{2}$

9 8 8 $9\frac{1}{2}$ 9 $9\frac{1}{2}$ $9\frac{1}{2}$ 10 8 $10\frac{1}{2}$ $7\frac{1}{2}$ 8

Complete this frequency table.

Shoe size	Tally	Frequency
6		
$6\frac{1}{2}$		
7		
$7\frac{1}{2}$		
8		
$8\frac{1}{2}$		
9		
$9\frac{1}{2}$		
10		
$10\frac{1}{2}$		
11		

2 A group of students played football every day after school. The table shows the number of goals scored each day.

Weekday	Mon	Tues	Wed	Thurs	Fri
Number of goals scored	8	4	6	3	5

Draw a bar chart to show this information.

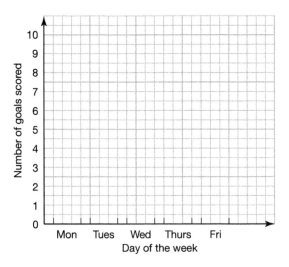

3 Given below are the marks of 60 students in an English test.

7 4 7 5 5 6 4 5 3 7

5 8 6 2 6 3 6 4 9 5

5 6 7 4 8 4 7 8 6 4

7 7 5 3 5 7 1 3 5 3

8 6 6 7 9 4 7 8 2 6

3 1 4 6 7 6 8 6 6 7

Using this data, complete the following grouped frequency table.

Mark	Tally	Frequency
1		
2		
3		
4		
5		
6		
7		
8		
9		

4 The following numbers show the number of people waiting at a shop checkout when they were counted at regular intervals throughout the day.

```
4  2  3  2  1  3  1  7  4  2
2  6  3  2  4  1  3  4  5  1
3  7  5  2  1  5  3  4  2  4
5  4  2  6  4  8  4  2  1  3
5  6  2  3  4  3  4  5  2  2
1  4  2  3  2  1  3  2  1  4
2  6  3  2  6  2  4  3  2  1
2  1  5  3  4  2  4  3  2  1
```

a How many counts were made?

_____

b Use this data to complete the following frequency table.

Mark	Tally	Frequency
1		
2		
3		
4		
5		
6		
7		
8		

5 Find the arithmetic average or mean of the following sets of numbers:

a 5, 11, 16, 24

_____

b 7.2, 8.3, 7.9, 8.1, 7.8

_____

c 0.49, 0.62, 1.03, 0.82, 0.97

_____

6 Find the mean and range of the following lists of numbers:

a 10, 16, 24, 12, 13, 15

Mean _____

Range _____

b 2.3, 2.2, 2.5, 2.2

Mean _____

Range _____

c 4, 7, 1, 7, 6, 5, 4, 2, 8, 6

Mean _____

Range _____

d 26.5, 37.9, 22.4, 36.1, 13.5

Mean _____

Range _____

7 Twenty-eight students took a science test and the average mark was 15. Joanie was away when the test was taken so sat it later. Her mark was 24.

a Will Joanie's mark increase or decrease the average mark for all the students who sat the test?

_____

b What is the total of the marks for all the students who took the test on the day?

_____

c What is the new mean mark when Joanie's mark is included?

_____

8 Wilf scored 3360 points in 32 visits to the dart board. Find his average number of points per visit.

_____

9 A rugby team scored 442 points in 26 league games. Find the average number of points per game.

10 A cricket team scored 2120 runs in the first ten games of the season. What was their average number of runs per game?

11 The recorded rainfall in Beachley last week was 0, 2.3 mm, 3.7 mm, 0, 0, 1.4 mm and 1 mm. Find the average daily rainfall for the week.

12 The family car will travel, on average, 53.4 miles on each gallon of petrol. How far will it travel on 25 gallons?

13 Eli's average mark in eight subjects was 64. After nine subjects it had increased to 67. How many marks had Eli scored in her ninth subject?

14 After 12 completed innings, Eddy had a batting average of 47. After 13 completed innings it had risen to 52. How many runs did Eddy score in his 13th innings?

15 During a certain week in Kingston, the numbers of hours of sunshine each day were 10.4, 12.0. 11.2, 11.7, 10.8, 10.3 and 11.0. The following week the daily average for the two weeks was 11.4 hours. How many more hours of sunshine were there in the second week than during the first week?

16 The average mass of 10 girls in a class of 25 students is 56.8 kg, while the average mass of the boys is 57.8 kg. Find the average mass of the pupils in the class.

17 Find the mode of each of the following sets of numbers:

a 8, 10, 12, 9, 12, 6, 10, 12, 14, 9, 7

b 43, 47, 44, 44, 47, 46, 44, 43

c 2.8, 2.7, 2.9, 2.9, 2.7, 2.5, 2.8, 2.7

18 The table shows the number of goals scored by a football team last season.

Number of goals	0	1	2	3	4	5	6
Frequency	10	9	14	8	0	1	2

Find the modal number of goals scored.

19 The number of letters in the words of a sentence were:

4, 3, 2, 7, 5, 4, 2, 7, 3, 4, 2, 3, 3,
9, 2, 5, 2, 6, 4, 2, 3, 5, 3, 2, 2, 5

a How many words were there in the sentence?

b What was the modal number of letters per word?

20 Find the median for each of the following sets of numbers:

  a 8, 3, 14, 7, 9, 12

  _____

  b 3.1, 4.2, 3.7, 5.9, 3.6, 3.2

  _____

  c 111, 98, 134, 103, 126, 72, 85, 132

  _____

21 Give the range for each set of numbers in question **20**.

  _____

22 The table shows the number of letters per word in a paragraph from Wendy's book.

Number of letters	1	2	3	4	5	6	7	8	9	10
Frequency	5	13	16	14	11	7	8	6	5	5

What is the range for this data?

  _____

23 The ages, in years, of the teenagers in a dance class are:

13, 16, 14, 15, 12, 13, 16, 14, 12, 14, 15, 14

  a Find:

   i the mean age

   _____

   ii the mode of the ages

   _____

   iii the median age.

   _____

  b One of the teenagers is chosen at random. What is the probability that this person is:

   i older than the mean age

   _____

   ii younger than the mean age?

   _____

24 Olivia measured the lengths of the six pencils in her pencil case. They were, in centimetres:

18.6, 18.2, 18.7, 18.2, 17.9, 18.2

  a Find:

   i the mean length   _____

   ii the modal length   _____

   iii the median length.   _____

The lengths of the pencils in Grant's pencil case were, in centimetres:

18.0, 17.4, 17.7 and 18.5

  b Find the mean length of Grant's pencils.

   _____

  c Find the mean length of Olivia's and Grant's pencils together.

   _____

25 A group of students were asked to count the number of books they were carrying. The distribution of their answers is shown in the bar chart.

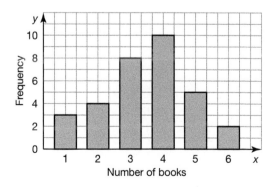

a How many students were asked?

_____

b Find the mode and the median number of books.

_____

c How many books did the students have altogether?

_____

d What was the mean number of books per student?

_____

In questions **26** to **31**, for each set of numbers find:

a the mean   **b** the mode

c the median   **d** the range

26 56, 57, 55, 53, 55, 52, 57, 59, 53, 53

a _____

b _____

c _____

d _____

27 18, 22, 3, 74, 83, 6, 3, 53, 35

a _____

b _____

c _____

d _____

28 83, 82, 82, 97, 96, 82, 87

a _____

b _____

c _____

d _____

29 65, 78, 65, 64, 65, 80, 69, 67, 68

a _____

b _____

c _____

d _____

30 12, 13, 16, 14, 15, 16, 14, 13, 17, 16, 17, 17, 14, 17, 16, 16, 12

a _____

b _____

c _____

d _____

31 107, 112, 107, 108, 107, 106, 107, 110

a _____

b _____

c _____

d _____

32 The marks out of 100 in a science test for the students in a class were:

46, 30, 50, 51, 46, 69, 50, 54, 47,

79, 43, 62, 48, 33, 83, 50, 45, 70,

29, 72, 47, 34, 42, 52, 50, 78, 44

Find:

a the mean mark   _____

b the modal mark   _____

c the median mark   _____

d the range.   _____

33 A six-sided die was rolled 40 times. The table gives the number of times each score was thrown.

Score	1	2	3	4	5	6
Frequency	6	4	5	6	11	8

Find:

a the mean score per throw

_____

b the mode.

_____

34 Jan counted the number of pencils each friend in a group had with them. The results are given in the table.

No. of pencils	0	1	2	3	4	5	6
Frequency	3	8	6	5	3	2	2

a How many friends were there in the group?

_____

b Find:

i the median   _____

ii the mode   _____

iii the mean.   _____

35 The table shows the number of plants bought by the customers at a garden centre.

No. of plants	1	2	3	4	5	6
Frequency	15	21	8	5	3	1

Find:

a the mean number of plants bought

_____

b the modal number.

_____

36 The table shows the numbers of workers at a plantation who were absent during the first two weeks of March.

No. of days absent	0	1	2	3	4	5	6	7	8	9	10
Frequency	33	4	1	1	3	5	0	2	0	0	1

Find:

a the mean

_____

b the mode

_____

c the median.

_____

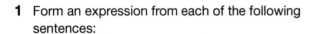

1 Form an expression from each of the following sentences:

a Think of a number and add 7.

_____

b Think of a number and subtract 4.

_____

c A number is multiplied by 5.

_____

d A number is 8 times an unknown number.

_____

2 Write sentences to show the meaning of each of the following expressions:

a $x - 6$ _____

b $n + 5$ _____

c $3n$ _____

d $12p$ _____

3 Simplify:

a $5x + 2x + 4x + 10x$

_____

b $5x - 3x + 6x - 3x$

_____

c $10x - 7x$

_____

d $10 - 4x - 3x + 6$

_____

4 Simplify:

a $5x + 6 - 3x - 4$

_____

b $3x + 5y + 7x + 2y$

_____

c $7x + 4y + 9x$

_____

d $9x + 6y - 4 + 3x - 5y$

_____

5 Multiply out the brackets:

a $3(x + 7)$ _____

b $4(2x + 5)$ _____

c $7(a + 2b)$ _____

d $5(6 + 4x)$ _____

6 Multiply out the brackets:

a $4(x + 1)$ _____

b $5(2x + 1)$ _____

c $3(4x + 2)$ _____

d $2(5x + 4)$ _____

e $3(7x + 3)$ _____

f $10(4 + 3x)$ _____

g $3(8x + 5)$ _____

7 Multiply out the brackets:

a $4(3x - 2)$ _____

b $6x(5 - 3x)$ _____

c $7x(4x + 3)$ _____

d $3(6x - 4)$ _____

8 Simplify:

a $3 + 4(x + 2)$ _____

b $5(2x + 1) + 4$ _____

c $6 + 3(4x + 3)$ _____

d $4x + 2(2x + 5)$ _____

e $7 + 3(3x + 2)$ _____

f $1 + 5(x + 3)$ _____

g $3(x + 1) + 9$ _____

h $6(3 + 2x) + 3x$ _____

i $4(2 + 3x) + x$ _____

j $5x + 2(4x + 1)$ _____

9 Simplify the following expressions:

a $4x + 3(x - 6)$ _____

b $3(2x + 1) + 5$ _____

c $8x + 2(4x - 3)$ _____

d $7 + 5(x - 5)$ _____

10 Simplify:

a $5x + 3(2x + 3)$ _____

b $4(3x - 2) + 10$ _____

c $8x + 3(3x - 2)$ _____

d $10x - 3(2 - 4x)$ _____

11 Write the following expressions in index form:

a $x \times x \times x \times x \times x$ _____

b $y \times y \times y \times y \times y \times y$ _____

12 Simplify the following expressions:

a $5 \times a$ _____

b $3 \times p \times y$ _____

c $x \times x \times y$ _____

d $2 \times x \times x \times 5$ _____

13 Write each expression without using indices:

a $4x^2$ _____

b $5y^3$ _____

c $3ab^2$ _____

d $5x^2y^3$ _____

14 Simplify the following expressions:

a $5x^2 \times x$ _____

b $a^2 \times a$ _____

c $3x \times 4y \times 2z$ _____

d $2x \times 3x$ _____

15 Find the value of $x - 9$ when:

a $x = 4$ _____

b $x = 7$ _____

c $x = -5$ _____

d $x = -9$ _____

16 Find the value of $20 - x$ when:

a $x = 9$ _____

b $x = -6$ _____

c $x = -12$ _____

d $x = -2$ _____

17 Find the value of $3x + 5$ when:

a $x = 2$ _____

b $x = 4$ _____

c $x = 6$ _____

d $x = 8$ _____

18 Find the value of $7 - 2x$ when:

a $x = 3$ _____

b $x = -2$ _____

c $x = -4$ _____

d $x = -5$ _____

19 Find the value of $5x - 3$ when:

a $x = 3$ _____

b $x = -3$ _____

c $x = -2$ _____

d $x = 6$ _____

20 Find the value of x^2 when:

   a $x = 4$ _____

   b $x = -4$ _____

   c $x = 7$ _____

   d $x = -7$ _____

21 Find the value of y^3 when:

   a $y = 3$ _____

   b $y = -2$ _____

   c $y = -4$ _____

   d $y = -5$ _____

22 Find the value of $3x^2$ when:

   a $x = 5$ _____

   b $x = -3$ _____

   c $x = -8$ _____

   d $x = -10$ _____

23 Given that $x = -3$ find the value of:

   a $2x^2$ _____

   b x^3 _____

   c $5x^2 + x$ _____

   d $3x^2 - 2x^3$ _____

24 Find the value of $\frac{a}{3}(a - 2)$ when $a = 5$.

_____

25 Find the value of $5xy$ when $x = 2$ and $y = -1$.

_____

26 Find the value of $\frac{x^2}{6}$ when $x = -4$.

_____

27 Find the value of $\frac{3x}{4} - \frac{2y}{3}$ when $x = 3$ and $y = 2$.

_____

28 Find the value of $b^2 - 4ac$ when $a = 4$, $b = 7$ and $c = 3$.

_____

29 Find the value of:

   a $3ab$ when $a = 2$ and $b = 3$

_____

   b $\frac{2}{5}(3x + 1)$ when $x = 3$

_____

   c $\frac{1}{2}(x^2 - 6)$ when $x = 4$

_____

   d $\frac{3x}{5} - \frac{2y}{3}$ when $x = 3$ and $y = 2$

_____

In questions **30** to **39**, choose the letter that gives the correct answer.

30 $4x - 2x + 8x + 5x$ simplifies to:

   A $13x$ **B** $14x$

   C $15x$ **D** $16x$

31 $5(4x - 3)$ simplifies to:

   A $20x - 3$ **B** $20x - 15$

   C $9x - 3$ **D** $9x - 15$

32 What does $6b^3$ mean?

   A $6 + b + b + b$ **B** $6 \times b \times b \times b$

   C $18b$ **D** none of these

33 $3a \times 4a \times 8a$ simplifies to:

   A $15a$ **B** $15a^3$

   C $48a^3$ **D** $96a^3$

34 The value of $5x^2$ when $x = 4$ is:

   A 20 **B** 25

   C 80 **D** 120

35 The value of $4xy$ when $x = -3$ and $y = 5$ is:

A −60 B −6

C 6 D 60

36 The value of $\dfrac{2}{x} + \dfrac{3}{y}$ when $x = 6$ and $y = 9$ is:

A $\dfrac{1}{3}$ B $\dfrac{5}{9}$

C $\dfrac{2}{3}$ D $\dfrac{7}{9}$

37 The value of $5(4 - x) + 3(5 - y)$ when $x = 2$ and $y = -1$ is:

A −8 B 8

C 24 D 28

38 The value of $4(5 - x) + 5(4 - y)$ when $x = 3$ and $y = -2$ is

A 22 B 32

C 38 D 42

39 The value of $\dfrac{2x}{3} + \dfrac{3y}{4}$ when $x = 4$ and $y = -2$ is:

A $-\dfrac{7}{6}$ B $\dfrac{6}{7}$

C 1 D $\dfrac{7}{6}$

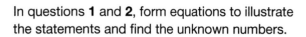

In questions **1** and **2**, form equations to illustrate the statements and find the unknown numbers.

1 a I think of a number, add 4 and get 11.

_____

   b I think of a number, subtract 6 and get 3.

_____

   c If 9 is subtracted from a number, we get 9.

_____

2 a I think of a number, treble it and get 15.

_____

   b If a number is multiplied by 4, we get 24.

_____

   c When we multiply a number by 7, we get 35.

_____

3 Write sentences to show the meaning of the following equations:

   a $5x = 30$

_____

   b $7 + x = 12$

_____

   c $x - 6 = 17$

_____

4 Solve the following equations:

   a $x + 4 = 9$ _____

   b $8 + a = 14$ _____

   c $y + 2 = 5$ _____

5 Solve the following equations:

   a $x - 9 = 5$ _____

   b $p - 4 = 11$ _____

   c $y - 7 = 3$ _____

6 Solve the following equations:

   a $6 = x + 3$ _____

   b $7 = x - 4$ _____

   c $x - 7 = 5$ _____

7 Solve the following equations:

   a $4x = 12$ _____

   b $5y = 8$ _____

   c $9x = 1$ _____

8 Solve the following equations:

   a $x - 8 = 10$ _____

   b $10 = x + 5$ _____

   c $6a = 36$ _____

9 Solve the following equations:

   a $5y = 2$ _____

   b $2x = 9$ _____

   c $x - 7 = 4$ _____

10 Solve the following equations:

   a $3x - 5 = 4$ _____

   b $7x + 1 = 15$ _____

   c $1 + 6p = 19$ _____

11 Solve the following equations:

   a $9x - 7 = 20$ _____

   b $5z + 6 = 7$ _____

   c $3x + 8 = 8$ _____

12 Solve the following equations:

a $3x = 12$ _____

b $x - 4 = 2x$ _____

c $3x + 4 = 10x$ _____

d $2 + 3x = 11x$ _____

e $4 + 8x = 20x$ _____

f $5x - 3 = 12x$ _____

13 Solve the following equations:

a $3x + 4 = 2x + 9x$ _____

b $x - 7 = 5 - x$ _____

c $x + 3 = 4x$ _____

d $3 - 3x = 7 - x$ _____

e $2x + 2 + 3x = 12$ _____

f $5 + x - 3 = 3x$ _____

14 Solve the following equations:

a $3x + 5 = 5x - 3$ _____

b $7x - 26 = 3x - 2$ _____

c $12 + 3x = 26 - 4x$ _____

15 Solve the following equations:

a $5x - 11 = 3 - 2x$ _____

b $2x - 6 = 3 - 7x$ _____

c $7 + x = 19 - 5x$ _____

16 Solve the following equations:

a $2x + 1 + 3x = 6$ _____

b $x - 3 + 7x = 1$ _____

c $2x + 7 - 4x + 1 = 4$ _____

d $6 - 2x - 4 = 17 - 5x$ _____

In questions **17** to **21**, form an equation to solve the problem.

17 I think of a number, multiply it by 3 and add 4. The result is 25. Find the number.

_____

18 I think of a number, multiply it by 5 and subtract 7. The result is 23. Find the number.

_____

19 When 5 is added to an unknown number the result is 19. What is the number?

_____

20 Two pieces of rope are each x m long. A third piece is 12 m long. Altogether the total length of the three pieces is 28 m. What is the length of the first two pieces?

_____

21 The lengths of the sides of a rectangle in order are x cm, $x + 4$ cm, x cm and $x + 4$ cm. The perimeter of the rectangle is 32 cm. Find:

a the lengths of the longer sides

_____

b the lengths of the shorter sides

_____

c the area of the rectangle.

_____

Solve the equations given in questions **22** to **30**.

22 $5 + 2(x + 3) = 15$

_____

23 $4(x + 2) = 20$

_____

24 $3x + 5(x + 2) = 34$

_____

25 $6x + 1 = 3x + 2(x + 1)$

_____

26 $2x + 3(2x + 1) = 19$

_____

27 $3 - (x - 2) = 3$

_____

28 $5 - (4 - x) = 8$

_____

29 $2(x - 4) + x - (3 - x) = 5$

_____

30 $4(2 - x) - 3(1 - 2x) = 11$

_____

31 Solve the following equations:

a $2(x + 2) = 10$

_____

b $2(3x - 1) = 10$

_____

c $3(3x - 7) = 2x + 7$

_____

d $6(x - 2) = 3x + 6$

_____

e $10(x - 2) = 5$

_____

f $3(1 + 2x) = 9$

_____

32 Solve the following equations:

a $28 = 4(3x + 1)$ _____

b $7x + (x - 3) = 21$ _____

c $8x - 3(2x + 3) = 1$ _____

d $6 = 5x - 2(x + 3)$ _____

e $x + 6 - 4(x - 3) = 0$ _____

f $3x - 1 = 4$ _____

33 I think of a number, double it and add 12. The result is 24. What is the number?

_____

34 I think of a number and add 8. The result is three times the first number. What is the number?

_____

35 I think of a number, treble it and add 10. The result is five times the first number. What is that number?

_____

36 A bus started from the terminus with x passengers. At the first stop another x passengers got on and 5 got off. At the next stop 10 passengers got on. There were then 21 passengers on the bus. How many were there on the bus to start with?

_____

37 When Sally went out for a meal, her starter cost $\$x$, the main course cost $1700 more than her starter, and her dessert cost twice as much as her starter. In total, the meal cost $5100. Find the cost of:

a her starter _____

_____

b her main course _____

_____

c her dessert. _____

_____

38 When Mrs Wesley went shopping she spent $x in the first shop and the same amount in the second shop. She spent $500 more in the third shop than she had spent in the first shop and $1200 more in the fourth shop than she had spent in the third shop.

The total she had spent in all four shops was $5000.

Form an equation in x and solve it.

_____

How much did she spend in:

a the first shop

_____

b the third shop

_____

c the fourth shop?

_____

39 The width of a rectangle is x cm. Its length is 5 cm more than its width.

The perimeter of the rectangle is 34 cm. Find its width.

_____

40 Stewart and Jen decide to visit a café. Stewart has a cup of tea and a cake and Jen has a cup of coffee and two cakes.
Coffee costs $50 more than tea and a cake costs $70 more than a cup of coffee.

a If a cup of tea costs $x, write down in terms of x, the cost of:

i a cup of coffee

_____

ii a cake

_____

iii two cakes.

_____

b The total cost of the tea, coffee and cakes is $1160. Form an equation in x and solve it.

Hence write down the cost of:

i a cup of tea

_____

ii a cup of coffee

_____

iii a cake.

_____

In questions **41** to **48**, choose the letter that gives the correct answer.

41 The solution of the equation $3x - 4 = 8$ is:

A 3   **B** 4

C 5   **D** 6

42 The solution of the equation $5x - 3 = 3x + 15$ is:

A 5   **B** 6

C 7   **D** 9

43 The solution of the equation $20 - 3x = 2$ is:

A 4   **B** 5

C 6   **D** 7

44 The solution of the equation $3x - 2 = 10$ is:

A 3   **B** 4

C 5   **D** 6

45 The value of x that satisfies the equation $4(2x - 3) - 2 = 3(x + 2)$ is:

A 1   **B** 2

C 3   **D** 4

46 The value of x that satisfies the equation $5(x - 2) - 2 = 2(x + 3)$ is:

A 6   **B** 7

C 8   **D** 9

47 I think of a number, treble it and add 3.
The answer is 18.
What number did I think of?

A 4   **B** 5

C 6   **D** 7

48 When I think of a number, double it and add 7, the result is three times the number I first thought of.
What number did I first think of?

A 4   **B** 5

C 6   **D** 7

In questions **1** to **17**, choose the letter that gives the correct answer.

1 The ratio 36 : 48 simplifies to:

   A 3 : 4   **B** 6 : 8

   C 9 : 12   **D** 18 : 24

2 The ratio 18 : 24 simplifies to:

   A 2 : 3   **B** 3 : 4

   C 4 : 3   **D** 8 : 6

3 In its simplest form the ratio 3.5 m to 145 mm is:

   A 7 : 29   **B** 70 : 29

   C 700 : 29   **D** 7000 : 29

4 If 2.94 m is divided into two parts in the ratio 5 : 9, the length of the longer part is:

   A 1.05 m   **B** 1.47 m

   C 1.68 m   **D** 1.89 m

5 A builder takes five days to build a wall 2 m high and 30 m long. The time he would take to build a similar wall 2.4 m high and with the same length would be:

   A $5\frac{1}{2}$ days   **B** 6 days

   C $6\frac{1}{2}$ days   **D** 8 days

6 The missing numbers in the ratios $\frac{3}{4} = \frac{}{12} = \frac{24}{}$ are:

   A 10 and 36   **B** 9 and 36

   C 9 and 32   **D** 12 and 32

7 The solution of the equation $5x + 2 + 3(4 - x) = 26$ is:

   A 4   **B** 6

   C 7   **D** 9

8 $5x + 1 - 2x + 4x - 6$ simplifies to:

   A $11x + 7$ **B** $7x + 5$

   C $7x - 5$ **D** $7x - 7$

9 If $9x - 5x - 2x - 4 = 0$, $x =$

   A 1   **B** 2

   C 3   **D** 4

10 I think of a number, multiply it by 3 and subtract 7. The answer is 38. The number I first thought of was:

   A 17   **B** 16

   C 15   **D** 14

11 $23x + 3y - 14x - 6y$ simplifies to:

   A $11x + 3y$ **B** $11x - 3y$

   C $9x + 3y$ **D** $9x - 3y$

12 $3(x + 2) + 5(2x + 3)$ simplifies to:

   A $13x + 2$ **B** $13x + 11$

   C $13x + 21$ **D** $8x + 17$

13 If $5x + 2(3x + 2) = 26$, $x =$

   A 1   **B** 2

   C 3   **D** 4

14 The value of x that satisfies the equation $3(x - 3) + 26 = 4(x + 3)$ is:

   A 5   **B** 6

   C 8   **D** 9

15 I think of a number, treble it and subtract 8. The result is 2 more than the number I first thought of. What number did I first think of?

   A 5   **B** 8

   C 9   **D** 12

16 Given that $R = a(b - c)$, the value of R when $a = 3$, $b = 5$ and $c = 2$ is:

A 12   **B** 9

C 6   **D** 3

17 Given that $X = 3(a + b)$, the value of b when $X = 54$ and $a = 4$ is:

A 12   **B** 14

C 16   **D** 18

18 Two lengths are in the ratio 3 : 8. The second length is 40 cm. What is the first length?

_____

19 Divide $4020 among three sisters in the ratio 4 : 7 : 9

_____

20 The map ratio of a map is 1 : 200 000. The distance between Portly and Quinton on the map is 7 cm. What is the true distance between these two towns?

_____

21 Divide $6240 in the ratio 7 : 9.

_____

22 The distances between four villages A, B, C and D, which lie in order along a north–south road, are such that AB : BC : CD = 5 : 3 : 7. If the distance from A to B is 15 km, find the distance:

a from B to C

_____

b from C to D

_____

c from A to D

_____

d from A to C.

_____

23 The map ratio of a map is 1 : 50 000. The distance between the towns of Westlake and Pennar is 12 kilometres. How far apart are they on the map?

_____

24 Simplify:

a $7(2x - 5)$

_____

b $13x + 5(3 - 2x)$

_____

c $2(7x - 2) - 3(4x + 1)$

_____

25 Simplify:

a $8x + 3y - 3x + 4y - 2x$

_____

b $6(3x - 5)$

_____

c $5x + 3(2x - 3)$

_____

d $4(3 - 5x) - 3(2 - 7x)$

_____

26 Find the value of $\frac{n}{2}(n + 1)$ when $n =$

a 7 _____

b 12 _____

c 20 _____

27 Find the value of $\dfrac{PRT}{100}$ when $P = 3000$, $R = 4$ and $T = 5$.

_____

28 I think of a number, double it and subtract 7. The result is 9. What is the number?

_____

29 Four brothers compared the number of books they had read.

Tony had read x books,

Pete had read $2x + 5$ books,

Derek had read $3x - 4$ books,

Ryan had read $3x + 2$ books.

The total number of books they had read between them was 75.

Form an equation in x and solve it.

_____

How many books had been read by:

a Tony _____

b Pete _____

c Derek _____

d Ryan _____

30 Solve the following equations:

a $x - 7 = 4$

_____

b $7x + 4 = 36 - x$

_____

c $5(x + 2) = 3(2x + 1)$

_____

d $3x + 5 + 4(x + 3) = 38$

_____

31 a A box contains N chocolates. I ate p of them and gave q chocolates to my best friend. Write down a formula for M, the number of chocolates left in the box.

_____

b Given that $I = \dfrac{PRT}{100}$, find R when $I = 30$, $P = 500$ and $T = 1\frac{1}{2}$.

_____

32 Edna and Ruth are sisters. Each of them has a box containing 20 chocolates. Edna eats 5 and gives some away to her friends. Ruth gives 1 away and eats three times as many as Edna has given away. When they compare their boxes, each sister has the same number of chocolates in her box as the other. If Edna gave x chocolates away, form an equation in x and solve it.

How many chocolates did Ruth eat?

_____

33 The average monthly rainfall for Sydney, Australia is given in the table.

Month	Jan	Feb	Mar	Apr	May	Jun
Rainfall (cm)	8.9	10.2	12.7	13.5	12.7	11.7
Month	Jul	Aug	Sept	Oct	Nov	Dec
Rainfall (cm)	11.7	7.6	7.4	7.1	7.4	7.4

a In which month does it:

  i rain least _____

  ii rain most? _____

b Draw a bar chart to represent this data.

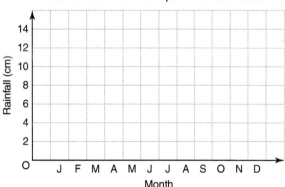

34 On the first six days of my holiday the daily rainfall figures were

0, 0, 5.2 mm, 1.3 mm, 0 and 1 mm.

a Find the mean daily rainfall for the first six days.

_____

b How much did it rain on the 7th day if the daily average for the week was 1.4 mm?

_____

35 This table shows the number of books borrowed from a public library one morning.

No. of books	1	2	3	4	5
Frequency	12	22	9	5	2

Find:

a the mean number of books borrowed

_____

b the modal number

_____

c the median.

_____

36 In a test, the marks out of 10 scored by the students in a music class are given in the table.

Mark	4	5	6	7	8	9	10
Frequency	5	8	7	5	3	1	1

a How many students are there in the class?

_____

b Find the range of these marks.

_____

c What is the modal mark?

_____

d Find the median mark.

_____

e Calculate the mean mark.

_____

37 The table shows the number of goals scored by the hockey first team in a season.

Number of goals	0	1	2	3	4	5	6
Frequency	14	18	96	6	4	2	3

a How many games did they play?

_____

b Find:

   i the mode

_____

   ii the median

_____

   iii the mean number of goals scored per match.

_____

c What is the range?

_____

38 Steepholm has an area of 50 000 hectares and last year the annual rainfall was 523 cm per hectare, while Flatholm has an area of 180 000 hectares and last year the annual rainfall was 234 cm per hectare. What was the annual rainfall last year for the combined area of Steepholm and Flatholm?

_____

15 Sets

1 Describe in words a set which includes the given members.

   a {January, February, March}

   _____

   b {France, Germany, Italy}

   _____

   c {II, IV, VI, X}

   _____

   d {a, b, c, d, e, f}

   _____

   e {Mandeville, Ocho Rios, Savanna-la-Mar, Spanish Town}

   _____

2 Describe a set which includes the given members and state another member of it.

   a {4, 8, 12, 16, 24}

   _____

   b {25, 9, 16, 1, 49}

   _____

   c {Paris, London, Rome}

   _____

   d {Nile, Amazon, Mississippi}

   _____

   e {Antigua, St Lucia, Jamaica}

   _____

3 List the members in each of these sets.

   a {prime numbers between 4 and 24}

   _____

   b {the letters used in the word 'Caribbean'}

   _____

   c {the last six letters of the alphabet}

   _____

   d {whole numbers greater than 12 but less than 25}

   _____

   e {whole numbers between 3 and 25 that are exactly divisible by both 3 and 4}

   _____

4 Write these statements in set notation.

   a Banana is a member of the set of fruit.

   _____

   b Mathematics is a member of the set of school subjects.

   _____

   c February is a member of the set of months of the year.

   _____

   d Garry Sobers is a member of the set of famous cricketers.

   _____

   e David Beckham is a member of the set of famous football players.

   _____

5 Write these statements in set notation.

a Panda is not a member of the set of fruit.

_____

b France is not a member of the set of Caribbean countries.

_____

c New York is not a member of the set of capital cities.

_____

d Sandal is not a member of the set of furniture.

_____

e Boeing is not a member of the set of motorcar manufacturers.

_____

6 Write down:

a two members that belong to

{rivers of the world}

_____

b two members that do not belong to

{rivers of the world}

_____

7 Write the following sentences in set notation.

a Chair is not a member of the set of cars.

_____

b Bee is a member of the set of living things.

_____

c Aeroplane is not a member of the set of boys' names.

_____

d Curtain is not a member of the set of floor coverings.

_____

e Argentina is a member of the set of South American countries.

_____

8 Write down the meaning of:

a cocoa $\in$ {beverages}

_____

b triangles $\notin$ {rectangles}

_____

c chemistry $\in$ {school subjects}

_____

d zebra $\notin$ {girls' names}

_____

In questions **9** to **11**, determine whether or not the given sets are equal.

9 A = {leg, arm, head, foot},
B = {head, foot, leg, arm}

_____

10 C = {odd numbers from 2 to 14 inclusive},
D = {3, 5, 7, 9, 13}

_____

11 E = {cities in the United Kingdom},
F = {Birmingham, Cardiff, Edinburgh, London, Manchester}

_____

12 Which of these are empty sets?

a {dogs with three legs}

_____

b {furniture made of ice cream}

_____

c {men with a mass more than 200 kg}

_____

d {cars with nine wheels}

_____

13 Suggest a suitable universal set for:

a {consonants}

_____

b {salamanders}

_____

c {subjects you are studying in school}

_____

14 If A = {p, q, r, s} write down all the subsets of A that have:

a two members

_____

b three members.

_____

15 If B = {5, 6, 7, ... 15} which of the following sets are subsets of B?

a {positive odd numbers less than 16}

_____

b {odd numbers between 4 and 16}

_____

c {prime numbers between 4 and 15}

_____

16 Write down two subsets, each with at least two members, for each of the following universal sets:

a {Caribbean countries}

_____

b {American states}

_____

c {rivers of the world}

_____

d {cities in the USA}

_____

17 Find the union of the two given sets:

a A = {2, 5, 7, 8}, B = {1, 2, 5, 6, 8, 9}

_____

b P = {p, q, r}, Q = {r, s, t, u}

_____

c D = {letters in the word 'programme'}
E = {letters in the word 'metre'}

_____

d J = {whole numbers that divide exactly into 15}
K = {whole numbers that divide exactly into 12}

_____

18 Draw suitable Venn diagrams to show the unions of the following sets:

  a $A = \{d, e, f, g\}, B = \{g, h, i, j\}$

  b $P = \{6, 9, 12, 15, 18\}, Q = \{6, 10, 14, 18, 22\}$

  c $R = \{$letters in the word 'Kingston'$\}$
      $S = \{$letters in the word 'Bridgetown'$\}$

  d $V = \{$odd numbers less than 14$\}$
      $W = \{$multiples of 3 less than 20$\}$

19 Find the intersection of the following pairs of sets:

  a $E = \{m, n, p, q, r\}, F = \{q, r, s, t, u\}$

  _____

  b $X = \{$prime numbers greater than 10 but less than 20$\}$
      $Y = \{$factors of 24$\}$

  _____

  c $T = \{$letters in the word 'Barbados'$\}$
      $U = \{$letters in the word 'Tobago'$\}$

  _____

  d $G = \{$Michelle, Denroy, Jasmine, Tenesha$\}$
      $H = \{$Henderson, Shevar, Michelle, Kaedron$\}$

  _____

20 Draw suitable Venn diagrams to show the intersections of the following sets:

  a $A = \{3, 6, 9, 12, 15\}$
      $B = \{4, 6, 8, 10, 12\}$

b C = {whole numbers less than 20}
D = {prime numbers less than 20}

c E = {letters in the word 'ancestor'}
F = {letters in the word 'descendant'}

21 Give the complement of each of the following sets:

a A = {4, 8, 10, 12}
U = {4, 6, 8, 10, 12, 14}

_____

b B = {Monday, Tuesday, Wednesday}
U = {days of the week}

_____

c P = {rectangles}
U = {quadrilaterals}

_____

22 Give the complement of each of the following sets:

a M = {female solicitors}
U = {solicitors}

_____

b X = {adults over 70 years old}
U = {adults}

_____

c C = {European cities}
U = {cities of the world}

_____

23 If A = {homes with a car} and
A' = {homes without a car}, what is U?

_____

24 If A = {a, b, c} and A' = {d, e, f} what is U?

_____

25 If A = {letters in the word JAMAICA} and
A' = {letters of the alphabet not in the word JAMAICA}, what is U?

_____

26 If P = {homes with a garden} and
P' = {homes without a garden}, what is U?

_____

27

Use this Venn diagram to list the following sets.

a A _____

b B _____

c $A \cup B$ _____

d $A \cap B$ _____

e $A' \cup B'$ _____

f $A' \cap B'$ _____

28 Use this Venn diagram to list the following sets:

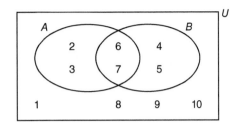

a A' _____

b B' _____

c $A \cup B$ _____

d the complement of $A \cup B$ _____

29 $U = \{1, 2, 3, 4, 5, 6, 7, 8, 9, 10, 11, 12\}$
$A = \{\text{factors of } 12\}$ and $B = \{\text{odd numbers}\}$

Show U, A and B on a Venn diagram. Hence list the sets:

a A' _____

b B' _____

c $A' \cup B'$ _____

d $A' \cap B'$ _____

30 $A = \{\text{numbers that divide exactly into } 30\}$
$B = \{\text{numbers that divide exactly into } 42\}$

List the members of:

a $A \cap B$ _____

b $A \cup B$ _____

31

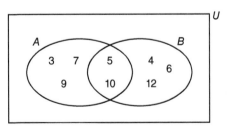

List the members of:

a A _____

b B _____

c $A \cup B$ _____

d $A \cap B$ _____

32 $U = \{3, 4, 5, 6, 7, 8, 9, 10, 11, 12,$
$13, 14, 15, 16, 17, 18, 19, 20\}$

$A = \{\text{prime numbers less than } 12\}$

$B = \{\text{prime numbers greater than } 6\}$

Show U, A and B on a Venn diagram.

Hence list the sets:

a A' _____

b B' _____

c $A \cup B$ _____

d $A' \cap B'$ _____

e $(A \cup B)'$ _____

f $A \cap B$ _____

33 Set A has 9 members and set B has 7 members. State:

a the largest possible number of members in set $A \cap B$ _____

b the smallest possible number of members in set $A \cap B$. _____

34 $S = \{\text{students wearing spectacles}\}$
$F = \{\text{students taller than } 140\,\text{cm}\}$

a Describe $S \cap F$.

_____

b Draw a Venn diagram and shade $S \cap F$.

38 B = {students with blue eyes}
D = {students shorter than 150 cm}

  a Describe $B \cap D$.

  _____

  b Draw a Venn diagram and shade $B \cap D$.

35 Set P has 10 members and set Q has 7 members. State:

  a the largest possible number of members in set $P \cap Q$

  _____

  b the smallest possible number of members in set $P \cap Q$.

  _____

  c Describe the set $B \cup D$.

  _____

36 Set A has 12 members and set B has 8 members. State:

  d Draw another copy of the Venn diagram and shade the region that represents the students who have blue eyes but are not shorter than 150 cm.

  a the largest possible number of members in set $A \cap B$

  _____

  b the smallest possible number of members in set $A \cap B$.

  _____

37 Give a subset with at least five members for each of the following sets:

  a {European countries}

  _____

  b {European capital cities}

  _____

  c {European rivers}

  _____

The bank notes currently in circulation in Jamaica have denominations of $50, $100, $500, $1000 and $5000. Use this information to answer questions **1** and **2**.

1 What is the smallest number of bank notes needed to make $9350?

_____

2 Give two possible mixtures of the lowest three denominations that can be used to make $1650.

_____

3 Bottles of a soft drink cost $150 each. How many can I buy for $2250?

_____

4 Coconut chocolate bars cost $65 each. Tony buys a bag full of them for $780 at the same unit price. How many bars are there in his bag?

_____

5 A bottle of my favourite hair shampoo costs $1050. A pack costs $6300. How many are there in the pack assuming that the unit price is the same?

_____

6 Find the cost of 12 bottles of a soft drink if they cost $220 a bottle.

_____

7 A jar of my favourite face cream costs $2160. A pack costs $17 280. How many jars are there in the pack?

_____

8 Find the cost of 12 bags of sweets at $135 each.

_____

9 Sam's ride to work costs $520 each way. How much does his travelling cost if he works a five-day week?

_____

10 A can of tinned fish costs $726 and contains 220 g of fish. What is the cost of:

a 1 g _____

b 50 g? _____

11 Nails of a given size are sold in packs of 100 for $315 and in packs of 50 for $164. Which pack is the better buy? Explain your answer.

_____

12 Rolls of wire are sold in two sizes: either 500 m for $2400 or 200 m for $1000. Pete said that the larger roll was the better value. Is Pete correct? Explain your answer.

_____

13 Which is the better buy: 75 g of coffee for $160 or 200 g for $370?

_____

14 Which is the better buy: a jar of chutney containing 350 g for $490 or a jar of the same chutney containing 250 g costing $325?

_____

15 In Cozumel supermarket, a 340 g jar of pickle costs $272. In Dante's supermarket a similar jar of pickle costs $185 for a 250 g jar. Which jar is the better buy? Explain your answer.

_____

In questions **16** to **19**, find the profit or loss.

16 A table costing $6120 is sold for $7956.

17 A telephone costing $10 380 is sold for $12 456.

18 A picture costing $139 200 is sold for $111 360.

19 A piece of furniture costing $8439 is sold for $9288.

In questions **20** and **21**, find the percentage profit.

20 Cost price $3600, profit $1080.

21 Cost price $4400, profit $2200.

In questions **22** and **23**, find the percentage loss.

22 Cost price $6000, loss $1200.

23 Cost price $8000, loss $1920.

In questions **24** to **27**, find the selling price:

24 Cost price $9400, profit 8%.

25 Cost price $4800, profit $12\frac{1}{2}$%.

26 Cost price $2240, loss 25%.

27 Cost price $4560, loss $37\frac{1}{2}$%.

28 A bicycle bought for $15 500 is sold at a profit of 20%. Find the selling price.

29 An article bought for $8500 is sold for $12 325. Find the percentage profit.

30 An article bought for $7600 is sold for $6460. Find the percentage loss.

31 A pack of three T-shirts bought for $4200 retails at $5040. Calculate the percentage profit.

32 A suite of furniture bought for $875 000 is sold for $52 500. Calculate the percentage loss.

Use the following exchange rates for questions **33** to **46**:

Jamaican dollars	$US	Barbadian dollars	UK pounds (£)
100	0.79	1.6	0.58

33 160 000 Jamaican dollars into US dollars.

34 2 370 000 Jamaican dollars into US dollars.

35 460 000 Jamaican dollars into UK pounds.

_____

36 950 000 Jamaican dollars into UK pounds.

_____

37 11 500 Jamaican dollars into Barbadian dollars.

_____

38 54 400 Jamaican dollars into Barbadian dollars.

_____

39 3950 US dollars into Jamaican dollars.

_____

40 2054 US dollars into Jamaican dollars.

_____

41 £464 into Jamaican dollars.

_____

42 £6612 into Jamaican dollars.

_____

43 US$4582 into UK pounds.

_____

44 £1160 into US dollars.

_____

45 3160 US dollars into Jamaican dollars.

_____

46 24 200 Jamaican dollars into UK pounds.

_____

47 Find the profit, or loss, given that:

a the cost price is $510 and the selling price is $620

_____

b the cost price is $3450 and the selling price is $3160

_____

c the cost price is $760 and the selling price is $530

_____

d the cost price is $1340 and the selling price is $1872.

_____

48 A garden centre bought 100 plants from a grower at $650 each. Eight plants arrived damaged and unfit for sale. The remainder were sold at $1250 each. Find:

a the cost of the plants to the garden centre

_____

b the total income from the sales

_____

c the total profit.

_____

49 Jewellery bought for $38 000 is sold for $62 700. Find the percentage profit.

_____

50 Jo bought a dining table and chairs for $250 000. He sold them again for $200 000. Find the percentage loss.

_____

51 A dealer sells a set of foreign postage stamps for $37 700. She makes a profit of $11 700. Find:

a how much she paid for them

_____

b her percentage profit.

_____

52 A retailer buys 250 articles for $112 500 and sells them for $400 each.

a Does he make a profit or a loss?

_____

b Express this profit (or loss) as a percentage.

_____

53 Suzie bought 45 soft toys for $24 300 and sold each one for $675. Find:

a Suzie's profit

_____

b her percentage profit.

_____

54 Diesel costs $185 a litre. How many complete litres can I buy for $5000?

_____

55 Jesse bought 30 identical picture frames at $246 each. He sold 26 of them at a profit of 15% and the remainder at a loss of 20%.

a What was his income from the frames he sold at a profit?

_____

b What was his income from the frames he sold at a loss?

_____

c Did Jesse make a profit or a loss on buying and selling the frames?

_____

d Justify your answer by finding his profit or loss.

_____

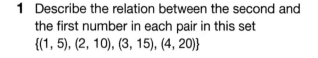

1 Describe the relation between the second and the first number in each pair in this set
{(1, 5), (2, 10), (3, 15), (4, 20)}

_____

2 Describe the relation between the second and the first number in each pair in this set
{(1, 4), (3, 6), (5, 8), (7, 10)}

_____

3 This table shows the name and number of CDs owned by three students.

Name	Number of CDs
Sally	20
Don	13
Victor	34

Write down the set of ordered pairs in the relation described as 'The second student in each pair has more CDs than the first.'

_____

4 Describe the relation between the second and first number in this set
{(2, 5), (3, 7), (4, 9)}

_____

5 The second number in each pair in this relation is the square of the first number. Fill in the missing numbers.

{(3, 9), (6, _____), (_____, 100)}

6 The second number in each pair in this relation is the next prime number that is larger than the first number. Fill in the missing numbers.

{(6, 7), (8, _____), (15, _____), (21, _____)}

7 The second number in each pair is this relation is four times the first number minus 1. Fill in the missing numbers

{(3, 11), (5, _____), (6, _____), (_____, 31)}

8 Write down the domain and range of the relation {(1, 4), (3, 6), (5, 8), (7, 10)}

_____

_____

9 Write down the domain and range of the relation {(1, 8), (3, 10), (5, 12), (7, 14)}

_____

_____

10 Write down the domain and range of the relation {(2, 6), (4, 8),(6, 10),(8, 12)}

_____

_____

11 The set {3, 5, 7} is the domain of a relation. The second number in each ordered pair is the square of the first. What is the range?

_____

12 Henderson, Stuart and Anthony are three boys. Stuart is heavier than Henderson and Anthony is heavier than Stuart.

a Write down the relation described as 'first boy in each pair is heavier than the second boy'.

_____

b Give the domain.

_____

c Give the range.

_____

13 Write down the domain and range of each relation.

a {(p, q), (p, r), (p, s), (r, t)}

_____

b {(1, 4), (2, 7), (3, 10), (4, 13)}

_____

14 Draw a mapping diagram to represent these relations.

a {(p, q), (p, r), (q, s)}

b {(2, 4), (3, 5), (6, 8), (10, 12)}

c {(3, 9), (5, 25), (9, 81), (10, 100)}

15 Draw the mapping diagram to represent the relation {(2, 4), (3, 7), (4, 10), (5, 13)}

16 Each diagram represents a relation. Write down the relation as a set of ordered pairs.

a

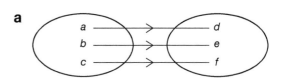

_____

b

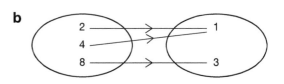

_____

c

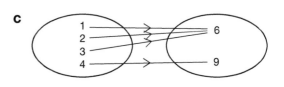

_____

17 Represent each relation as a table of values of _x_ and _y_, and illustrate them on a graph.

a {(1, 3), (2, 5), (3, 7), (4, 9)}

x	1	2	3	4
y				

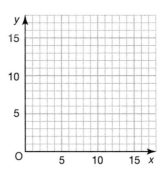

b {(3, 1), (6, 2), (9, 3), (12, 4)}

x				
y				

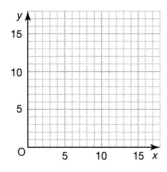

c {(12, 9), (10, 7), (9, 6), (5, 2)}

x				
y				

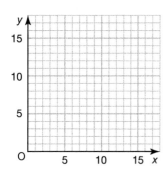

18 This diagram represents a relation. Write the relation as a set of ordered pairs.

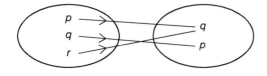

_____

19 Represent each relation as a table of values of x and y and illustrate them on a graph. In each case state the type of relation represented.

a (0, 8), (2, 6), (5, 5), (6, 2)

b (2, 1), (4, 2), (6, 3), (8, 4)

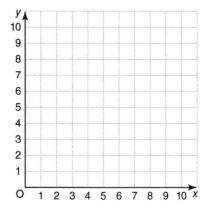

20 A relation is represented by this table.

x	0	0	4	−4
y	−4	4	0	0

a Illustrate this relation on a graph.

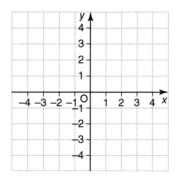

b Do all these points lie on a straight line?

_____

c What type of relation is this?

_____

21 A relation is represented by this table.

x	4	6	10
y	2	3	5

   a Illustrate the relation on a graph.

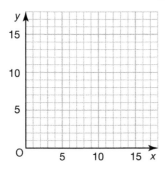

   b What type of relation is this?

_____

22 Represent this relation as a table of values of x and y.

{(0, 2), (1, 3), (2, 6), (3, 11), (4, 18)}

x					
y					

23 The table represents a relation.

x	2	2	3	5	5
y	5	7	9	13	18

What type of relation is this? Give a reason for your answer.

_____

24 This graph illustrates a relation.

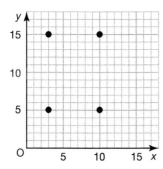

a Represent the relation as a table.

x				
y				

b Give the relation as a set of ordered pairs.

_____

c What type of relation is this?

_____

25 The points A, B, C and D illustrate a relation.

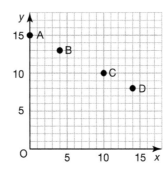

   a Represent these points as a table.

	A	B	C	D
x				
y				

   b How is the y-coordinate of each point related to the x-coordinate?

_____

   c The points A, B, C and D all lie on the same straight line. E is another point on this line. Its x-coordinate is 12. What is its y-coordinate?

_____

   d What type of relation is this?

_____

26 The graph illustrates a relation.

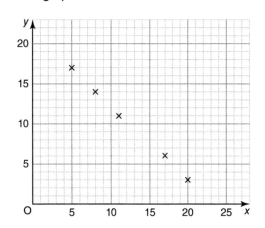

a Represent the relation as a table.

x					
y					

b Give the relation as a set of ordered pairs.

_____

c What type of relation is this?

_____

27 The points A, B, C, D and E illustrate a relation.

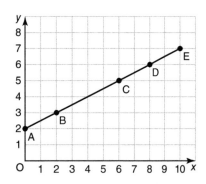

a Represent these points as a table.

	A	B	C	D	E
x					
y					

b How is the y-coordinate of each point related to the x-coordinate?

_____

c The points A, B, C, D and E all lie on the same straight line. F is another point on the line. Its x-coordinate is 4. What is its y-coordinate?

_____

d G, H and I are three other points on the line. Find the missing coordinates.

(12, _____), (14, _____), (a, _____)

28 A relation is given by {(x, y)} where

y = 4x for x = 1, 2, 3.

Complete this table of values.

x	1	2	3
y		8	

29 A relation is given by {(x, y)} where

y = 15 − 3x for x = 1, 2, 3 and 5.

Complete this table of values.

x	1	2	3	4
y		9		

30 A relation is given by {(x, y)} where
$y = 4x - \frac{1}{2}$ for x = 0, 1, 2, 3.

Complete the table.

x	0	1	2	3
y				

31 A relation is given by {(x, y)} where
$y = 4x - \frac{1}{2}$ for $x = 1, 1\frac{1}{2}, 2, 2\frac{1}{2}$.

a Complete the table.

x	1	$1\frac{1}{2}$	2	$2\frac{1}{2}$
y		$5\frac{1}{2}$		

b Write down the domain and range

_____

c Represent the relation with an arrow diagram.

d What type of relation is this?

---

32 A relation is given by {(x, y)} where

$y = 3 + x^2$ for $x = 1, 2, 3, 4$.

Complete this table of values.

x	1	2	3	4
y			12	

33 A relation is given by {(x, y)} where

$y = x^2 + 3x - 4$ for $x = 1, 2, 3, 4$.

Complete this table of values.

x	1	2	3	4
y			14	

34 A relation is given by {(x, y)} where

$y = 2x^2 - x$ for $x = 1, 2, 3, 4$.

Complete this table of values.

x	1	2	3	4
y		6		

35 A relation is given by {(x, y)} where

$y = x^3 - x^2 + 4$ for $x = 0, 1, 2, 3$.

Complete this table of values.

x	0	1	2	3
y			8	

In questions **36** to **43**, choose the letter that gives the correct answer.

36 The relation between the first number and the second number in each of the pairs in the set (2, 1), (3, 3), (4, 5), (5, 7), (6, 9) is:

A Double the first and subtract 3

B Double the first and add 3

C Treble the first and subtract 5

D Treble the first and subtract 6

37 The second number in each pair in the following relation is double the first and then subtract 2:

(2, 2), (4,   ), (7, 12)

The missing number is:

A 4   **B** 6

C 8   **D** 10

38 The domain of {(2, 4), (4, 7), (5, 9), (6, 11)} is:

A {2, 3, 4, 5, 6}

B {2, 4, 5, 6}

C {2, 3, 5, 6}

D {2, 3, 4, 6}

39 The range of the relation {(3, 12), (4, 16), (5, 20), (6, 24)} is:

A {2, 3, 4, 5, 6}

B {3, 4, 5, 6}

C {12, 16, 20, 24}

D {2, 4, 5, 6, 12, 16, 20, 24}

40 What type of relation is this?

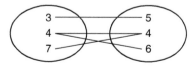

A 1 : 1   **B** 1 : n

C n : 1   **D** n : n

41 The table represents a relation.

x	1	2	3	6
y	7	5		-3

The missing number from this table is

A 6

B 4

C 3

D -3

42 The table represents a relation.

x	2	4	3	6	8
y	1	3	2	3	1

What type of relation is this?

A 1 : 1

B 1 : n

C n : 1

D n : n

43 A relation is given by {(x, y)} where $y = 6 - 3x$ for $x = 1, 2, 4, 6$.

x	1	2	4	6
y	3		-6	-12

The missing number is:

A 0

B 1

C 2

D 3

1

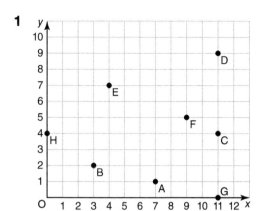

Write down the coordinates of the points:

A(,   ),   B(,   ),
C(,   ),   D(,   ),
E(,   ),   F(,   ),
G(,   ),   H(,   ).

2

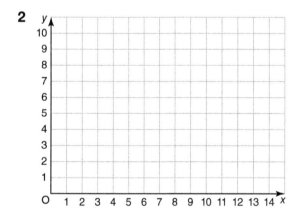

Mark the points:
A(2, 3), B(10, 6),
C(7, 10), D(3, 7),
E(14, 2), F(12, 0),
G(8, 3), H(8, 1).

Join the points in alphabetical order and then join A to H.

3

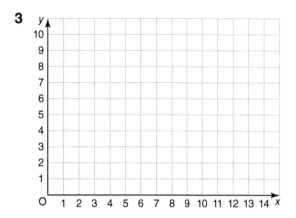

Mark the following points on the grid:
A(3, 1), B(3, 5),
C(10, 5), D(10, 1).

Join A to B, B to C, C to D and D to A.

What is the name of the figure ABCD?

_____

4

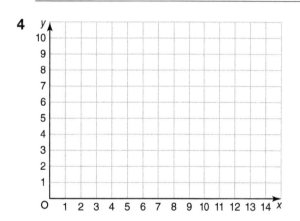

Mark the following points on the grid:
A(2, 6), B(9, 8),
C(11, 4), D(4, 2).

Join A to B, B to C, C to D and D to A.

What is the name of the figure ABCD?

_____

5

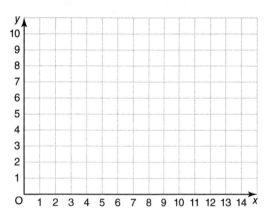

Mark the following points on the grid:
A(2, 9), B(12, 9),
C(10, 3), D(4, 3).

Join A to B, B to C, C to D and D to A.

What is the name of the figure ABCD?

_____

7

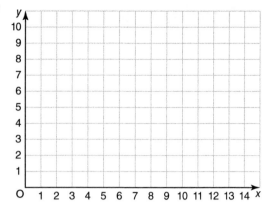

Mark the points:
A(3, 2), B(2, 7), C(7, 8),
D(12, 7), E(11, 2).

Describe the shape ABCDE.

_____

6

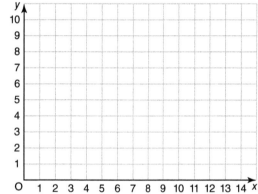

Mark the points:
A(2, 6), B(11, 9), C(14, 0).

What type of triangle is ABC?

_____

8

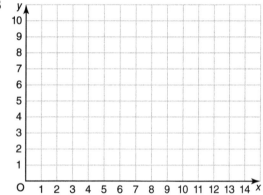

Mark the points:
A (3, 5), B (6, 8), C (9, 5), D(6, 2).

Describe the shape ABCD.

_____

9

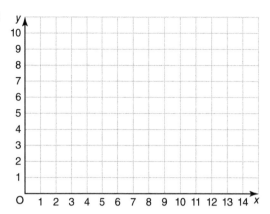

a The points A(2, 1), B(7, 1) and C(7, 9) are three of the vertices of a rectangle ABCD.

Mark the points A, B and C.
Find the point D and write down its coordinates.

_____

b E is a point on BC and F is a point on AD such that ABEF is a square. Mark E and F on your diagram and write down the coordinates of E and F.

_____

10

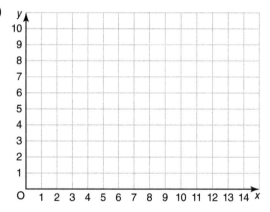

The points A(6, 2), B(2, 7) and C(10, 9) are three of the vertices of a parallelogram.
Mark the points A, B and C.
Find the point D and write down its coordinates.

_____

11

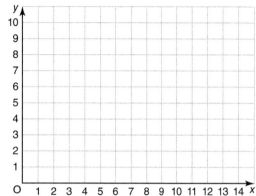

The points A(2, 2), B(2, 7) and C(12, 2) are the vertices of a triangle ABC.

Plot these points and mark D, the midpoint of AB, E the midpoint of AC and F the midpoint of BC.
Write down the coordinates of D, E and F.

D _____

E _____

F _____

What is special about triangle ABC?

_____

Does triangle DEF have the same property?

_____

12

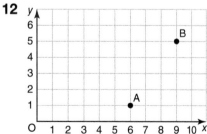

a Write down the coordinates of A and B.

A _____ B _____

b Plot the points C(4, 5) and D(1, 1).

c Join the points in order to give quadrilateral ABCD.

d Measure all four sides. What special name do we give to this quadrilateral?

_____

e How many lines of symmetry does this quadrilateral have?

_____

f Does the quadrilateral have rotational symmetry?

_____

g If your answer is 'yes', give the order of rotational symmetry.

_____

13

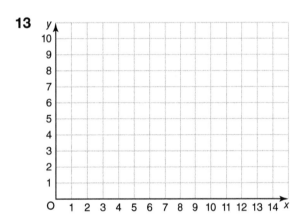

a Plot the points P(3, 9), Q(13, 9), R(9, 1).

b Mark S, the midpoint of RQ, and write down its coordinates.

_____

c Measure the lengths of the three sides of the triangle.

PQ = _____

PR = _____

QR = _____

d What special name do we give to this triangle?

_____

e Mark T, the midpoint of PR and U, the midpoint of ST.

Write down the coordinates of U.

_____

14 a Draw x and y axes and mark each axis from –6 to 6.

b Plot the points A(4, –3), B(5, 4), C(–2, 3) and D(–3, –4).

c What type of quadrilateral is this?

_____

d Join A to C and B to D. Mark the point where these diagonals cross E.

e Is E the midpoint of either, both, or neither of the diagonals?

_____

f Measure the four angles at E. Do the diagonals cross at right angles?

_____

15 Repeat question **14** for the points A(6, –5), B(5, 3), C(–3, 2) and D(–2, –6).

16 Repeat question **14** for the points A(–3, 3), B(3, 2), C(–5, 2) and D(–5, –3).

17 Find the *y*-coordinates of points on the line *y = x* that have *x*-coordinates of:

a 1 _____   **b** –2 _____

c –6 _____   **d** 10 _____

18 Find the *y*-coordinates of points on the line *y = –x* that have *x*-coordinates of:

a 4 _____   **b** –5 _____

c 2.5 _____   **d** 4.3 _____

19 Find the *x*-coordinates of points on the line *y = –2x* that have *y*-coordinates of:

a 8 _____   **b** –2 _____

c 3.5 _____   **d** –6.4 _____

20 Find the *y*-coordinates of points on the line *y = 3x* that have *x*-coordinates of:

a 3 _____   **b** –4 _____

c –5.5 _____   **d** 2.4 _____

21 Find the *x*-coordinates of points on the line $y = \frac{1}{2}x$ that have *y*-coordinates of:

a 8 _____   **b** 7 _____

c 0.8 _____   **d** –3.8 _____

22 Find the *x*-coordinates of points on the line *y = –5x* that have *y*-coordinates of:

a 20 _____   **b** –15 _____

c 6 _____   **d** –3 _____

23 Using the same scale on each axis plot the points (–6, 4), (0, 0), (3, –2) and (6, –4). What is the equation of the straight line that passes through these points?

_____

24 Which of the points (2, 3), (3, 2), (6, 9) and (9, 6) lie on the line $y = \frac{2}{3}x$?

_____

25 Which of the points (2, –4), (4, 8), (–5, –10) and (7, –14) do not lie on the line *y = –2x*?

_____

26 Which of the points (2, 6), (3, 6), (4, –8), (6, 3), (2, 8) and (4, –2) lie on these lines:

a *y = 2x* _____

b *y = 4x* _____

c $y = -\frac{1}{2}x$? _____

27 Plot the graph of $y = 2x$.

Does the point (2, 4) lie on this line?

_____

28 Plot the graph of $y = -2x$.

Does the point (4, −1) lie on this line?

_____

29 Plot the graph of $y = \frac{2}{3}x$.

Does the point (3, 1) lie on this line?

_____

30 Plot the graph of $y = -\frac{1}{2}x$.

Does the point (4, −2) lie on this line?

_____

31 Which of the straight lines whose equations are:

$$y = 3x, \ y = \frac{1}{2}x, \ y = -3x, \ y = \frac{4}{3}x \ \text{ and } \ y = 9x$$

  a make an obtuse angle with the positive x-axis

  _____

  b make an acute angle with the positive x-axis?

  _____

32 Consider the special quadrilaterals: rectangle, square, kite, rhombus and parallelogram.

  a In which quadrilateral(s) do the diagonals intersect at right angles?

  _____

  b In which quadrilateral(s) are the lengths of the two diagonals equal?

  _____

19 Volume and capacity

1 Express 4 cm^3 in:

  a mm^3 _____

  b m^3 _____

2 Express 0.005 m^3 in:

  a mm^3 _____

  b cm^3 _____

3 Express 8000 mm^3 in:

  a m^3 _____

  b cm^3 _____

4 Express 5600 cm^3 in litres.

_____

5 Express 0.75 litres in cm^3.

_____

6 Express:

  a 8 cm^3 in mm^3 _____

  b 0.55 cm^3 in mm^3 _____

  c 0.1 cm^3 in mm^3 _____

  d 850 mm^3 in cm^3 _____

  e 4000 mm^3 in cm^3 _____

  f 95 000 mm^3 in cm^3 _____

7 Express:

  a 1.75 litres in cm^3 _____

  b 0.45 litres in cm^3 _____

  c 0.006 litres in cm^3 _____

  d 36 000 cm^3 in litres _____

  e 860 cm^3 in litres _____

  f 120 cm^3 in litres _____

In questions **8** to **13**, find the volume of each of the cuboids with the given dimensions.

	Length	Breadth	Height	Volume
8	5 cm	4 cm	3 cm	
9	12 mm	8 mm	2.4 mm	
10	4.3 m	3 m	1.2 m	
11	3.5 m	2.2 m	0.8 m	
12	12 cm	8 cm	5 cm	
13	20 mm	10 mm	8 mm	

In questions **14** to **22**, find the volume of a cube with a side of length:

14 8 cm _____

15 $\frac{3}{4}$ m _____

16 5 mm _____

17 0.6 m _____

18 $\frac{1}{4}$ cm _____

19 $1\frac{3}{4}$ m _____

20 12 mm _____

21 5.5 cm _____

22 4.3 m _____

In questions **23** to **28**, find the volume of each of the cuboids whose dimensions are given.

Give each answer in the units in brackets.

	Length	Breadth	Height	Volume
23	40 mm	30 mm	20 mm	(cm^3)
24	500 cm	200 cm	80 cm	(m^3)
25	5 cm	30 mm	14 mm	(mm^3)
26	0.5 m	35 cm	20 cm	(cm^3)
27	0.5 m	66 cm	40 cm	(cm^3)
28	10 m	800 cm	50 cm	(m^3)

29 Find the volume of air in a room measuring 5 m by 6 m which is 3.5 m high.

30 How many cubic metres of water are required to fill a swimming rectangular pool measuring 20 metres by 12 metres, and which is 2 metres deep throughout? Convert your answer to litres.

31 A box measures 12 cm by 9 cm by 6 cm. How many cubes of side 3 cm will fit into this box?

32 A cubical box has a capacity of 1 m³. How many cubes of side 20 cm will fit into this box?

33 A water storage tank will hold 9000 litres of water. The tank is 3 m long and 2 m wide. How deep is it?

34 A carton measures 15 cm by 8 cm by 6 cm. What is the maximum number of boxes measuring 5 cm by 4 cm by 3 cm that will fit into the carton?

35 The area of one side of a cube is 9 cm. How many such cubes would fit into a carton measuring 15 cm by 18 cm by 12 cm?

36 A rectangular water-tank measures 5 m by 3.5 m by 60 cm. Calculate the capacity of the tank:

a in cubic metres

b in litres.

37 How many rectangular packets measuring 6 cm by 4 cm by 3 cm can be packed into a rectangular metal box measuring 24 cm by 16 cm by 12 cm?

38 A rectangular fuel tank is 2 m long, $1\frac{1}{2}$ m wide and 1 m deep. How many litres of fuel will it hold?

39 How many metal cubes of side 8 mm can be made from a rectangular block of metal measuring 16 cm by 8 cm by 4 cm?

40 Find the volume, in cubic centimetres, of a cuboid measuring 80 cm by 6.5 m by 60 cm. How many cubic metres is this?

1 Describe the following sets in words:

  a {March, April, May}

  _____

  b {cups, mugs, beakers, glasses}

  _____

2 List the members in the following sets:

  a {prime numbers between 25 and 35}

  _____

  b {the letters used in the word 'multiplication'}

  _____

3 Write the following statements in set notation:

  a December is not a day of the week.

  _____

  b Saturday is a day of the week.

  _____

  c Hexagon is not a member of the set of living things.

  _____

  d A table is a piece of household furniture.

  _____

4 Determine whether or not the sets
A = {trousers, coat, shoe, jacket} and
B = {shirt, jacket, blouse, coat}
are equal.

_____

5 Determine whether or not the sets
P = {11, 3, 7, 5, 2} and
Q = {prime numbers less than 12}
are equal.

_____

6 Which of the following sets are empty:

  a {pigs with wings} _____

  b {horses with four legs} _____

  c {cats with three legs} _____

In questions **7** and **8**, describe a set which includes the given members and state another member of it.

7 Colin, Elsie, John, Wendy

_____

8 Christiana, Portmore, Mandevilla, Spanish Town

_____

9 Suggest a universal set for:

  a {20, 25, 30, 35, 40}

  _____

  b {rugby players, hockey players, golfers, hurdlers}

  _____

10 Find the intersection of the following pairs of sets:

  a A = {p, q, r, s, t}, B = {l, m, n, o, p}

  _____

  b D = {letters in the word 'father'},
    E = {letters in the word 'mother'}

  _____

11 Draw a Venn diagram to show the intersection of the sets:
A = {letters in the word 'satchel'},
B = {letters in the word 'literacy'}

12 Draw a Venn diagram to show the intersection of the sets:
$P = \{\text{factors of } 18\}$, $Q = \{\text{factors of } 20\}$

13 $U = \{\text{positive integers from 1 to 12 inclusive}\}$

  a List the following sets:

    i $A = \{\text{even numbers from 1 to 12 inclusive}\}$

_____

    ii $B = \{\text{prime numbers less than 12}\}$

_____

    iii $C = \{\text{multiples of 4 less than or equal to 12}\}$

_____

  b Write down:

    i $A \cup B$ _____

    ii $A \cap B$ _____

  c Find:

    i $n(A \cup B)$ _____

    ii $n(A \cap B)$ _____

14

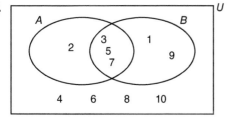

  a Describe in words:

    i the universal set

_____

    ii set A

_____

    iii set B

_____

  b Find:

    i $n(A \cup B)$

_____

    ii $n(A \cap B)$

_____

15 The cost of 12 bags of tea is $126. What is the cost of:

  a 1 bag

_____

  b 5 bags?

_____

16 Rolls of kitchen paper are sold in two different pack sizes: packs of 9 costing $1296 and packs of 12 costing $1836. Which pack is the better value for money? Justify your answer.

_____

_____

17 Find the profit (or loss) if:

  a a computer bought for $46 000 is sold for $57 500

_____

  b a car costing $2 960 000 is sold for $2 158 999.

_____

18 An article bought for $16 000 is sold for $20 000. Find the percentage profit.

19 Mellie bought an antique jug for $58 500 and sold it some years later for $49 725. Find:

   a how much she lost on the deal

   _____

   b her percentage loss.

   _____

20 If the equivalent of $100 Jamaican dollars is US$0.82 and UK£0.63 convert the following. (Give your answers to **a** and **b** correct to the nearest whole number and **c** and **d** correct to the nearest $100.)

   a Jam$65 000 into US dollars

   _____

   b Jam$85 000 into UK pounds

   _____

   c £750 into Jamaican dollars

   _____

   d US$1000 into Jamaican dollars

   _____

21 Write the domain and range of the relation {(2, 5), (3, 7), (5, 11), (7, 15)}

   _____

22 Represent the relation {(0, 0), (1, 5), (4, 7), (5, 11), (6, 5)} as a table of values of x and y. What type of relation is this?

   _____

23 A relation is given by {(x, y)} where $y = x^2 - 3x + 5$ for $x = 1, 2, 3, 4$.

   a Complete the following table.

x	1	2	3	4
y		3	5	

   b Write down the domain and range.

   _____

   c Represent the relation with an arrow diagram.

   d What type of relation is this?

   _____

24 Draw axes for x and y from –3 to 10. On these axes plot the points P(0, –3), Q(10, 1), R(8, 6), S(–2, 2)

a What type of quadrilateral is PQRS?

_____

b Draw the diagonals and mark the point where they cross T.

_____

c Measure the diagonals. Are the diagonals the same length?

_____

d Is T the midpoint of either, or both, of the diagonals?

_____

e Do the diagonals cross at right angles?

_____

25 Find the y-coordinates of the points on the line $y = 3x$ that have x-coordinates of:

a –3 _____ **b** 0 _____

c 3 _____ **d** 0.5 _____

26 Which of the points A(–1, 6), B(2, 3), C(3, 4), D(6, –1) lie on the line $y = 5 – x$?

_____

27

a Write down the coordinates of A, B and C.

A(,   )

B(,   )

C(,   )

b Mark and label the point D so that all the sides in the quadrilateral ABCD are the same length.

c What name do we give to this type of quadrilateral?

_____

d How many lines of symmetry does ABCD have?

_____

28 Express in cm^3:

a $1.5 m^3$ _____

b $60\,000 mm^3$ _____

c $0.002 m^3$ _____

29 A cuboid measures 15 cm by 240 cm by 8 cm. Find its volume:

a in cm^3 _____

b in m^3 _____

30 a Find the volume of a cube with a side of 12 cm.

_____

b Find the volume of a cuboid with dimensions 12 cm by 25 mm by 8 mm. Give your answer in cm^3.

_____

31 A rectangular oil tank is 2 m long and 2.5 m wide.

a If it is 1.5 m deep, what is the maximum amount of oil it will hold? Give your answer in litres.

_____

b If the tank is empty and 5000 litres of oil is fed into it, to what height will the oil level rise?

_____

32 How many cubes of side 6 cm will fit into a rectangular carton measuring 36 cm by 24 cm by 18 cm?

_____

In questions **33** to **40**, choose the letter that gives the correct answer.

33 Given that $P = \{2, 5, 7, 9\}$ and $U = \{1, 2, 3, 4, 5, 6, 7, 8, 9, 10\}$, the complement of P is:

A $\{1, 3, 6, 8, 10\}$ **B** $\{1, 3, 4, 6, 10\}$

C $\{1, 3, 4, 8, 10\}$ **D** $\{1, 3, 4, 6, 8, 10\}$

34 $U = \{1, 2, 3, 4, 5, 6, 7, 8, 9, 10, 11, 12\}$
$P = \{$multiples of 3$\}$
$Q = \{$prime numbers$\}$
$(P \cup Q)'$ is:

A $\{3\}$

B $\{2, 3, 5, 6, 7, 9, 11, 12\}$

C $\{1, 4, 6, 8, 9, 10, 12\}$

D $\{1, 4, 8, 10\}$

35 An article bought for $8440 and sold for $8862 gives the seller a profit of:

A 5%   **B** 10%

C 15%   **D** 20%

36 When the exchange rate is $100 Jamaican dollars is equivalent to 1.61 Barbadian dollars, the equivalent of $550 Barbadian in Jamaican dollars is, correct to the nearest $100:

A $34 200   **B** $34 000

C $34 380   **D** $88 600

37 A relation is given by $\{x, y\}$ where $y = 5x - 4$. For $x = 2$, $y =$

A 2   **B** 4

C 6   **D** 8

38 What special name is given to the quadrilateral that has the following properties:

Its opposite sides are equal,
its diagonals are equal and
its diagonals do not intersect at right angles.

A parallelogram   **B** square

C rhombus   **D** trapezium

39 Expressed in litres 0.046 m³ is:

A 0.46   **B** 4.6

C 46   **D** 460

40 This solid is made by fixing a square pyramid to one face of a cube.

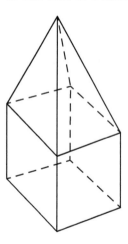

The number of faces this solid has is:

A 8   **B** 9

C 10   **D** 11

1 Write 52 649 as:

   a an approximate number of tens

   _____

   b an approximate number of hundreds

   _____

   c an approximate number of thousands

   _____

   d an approximate number of tens of thousands.

   _____

2 At 7 am the temperature was –7°C. At 2 pm it was 9°C warmer. What was the temperature at 2 pm?

_____

3 a Subtract 4 from –9

   _____

  b Add –3 to –5

   _____

  c Find three times –7

   _____

  d Calculate $2(5 + 3) \div 8 \times (7 - 5)$

   _____

4 a Which fraction is the larger, $\frac{11}{13}$ or $\frac{13}{18}$?

   _____

  b Which fraction is the smaller, $\frac{5}{7}$ or $\frac{7}{9}$?

   _____

  c Find $\frac{7}{12} + \frac{1}{3} + \frac{1}{2}$

   _____

  d Find $7\frac{3}{4} - 2\frac{5}{8}$

   _____

5 In a group of 60 girls, $\frac{1}{3}$ play hockey, $\frac{2}{5}$ play netball, $\frac{1}{6}$ play both games, while the remainder play neither game. How many play:

   a hockey

   _____

  b netball

   _____

  c both sports

   _____

  d hockey but not netball

   _____

  e netball but not hockey

   _____

  f neither sport?

   _____

6 Find:

   a $4.56 - 2.93 + 5.87$

   _____

  b $1.82 \div 7$

   _____

  c 0.79×0.6

   _____

7 Calculate, giving your answers correct to three decimal places:

  a $0.6494 \div 18$

  _____

  b $1.427 \div 23$

  _____

  c $4.64 \div 2.51$

  _____

8 Out of 30 applicants for a post at the local supermarket, six were offered a position. What percentage was this?

  _____

9 In a school with 440 students 55% are boys. How many more boys than girls are there?

  _____

10 Put either > or < between the following pairs of fractions:

  a $\dfrac{5}{8}$ $\qquad$ $\dfrac{6}{11}$

  b $\dfrac{7}{15}$ $\qquad$ $\dfrac{5}{12}$

  c $\dfrac{3}{7}$ $\qquad$ $\dfrac{6}{13}$

11 Express the given quantity in terms of the unit in brackets:

  a 0.075 m (mm) _____

  b 5.4 g (mg) _____

  c $2\frac{3}{4}$ hours (minutes) _____

  d 475 g (kg) _____

12 Find the area of each of the given rectangles. Give your answer in the unit in brackets.

  a A rectangle measuring 40 mm by 6 cm (cm^2)

  _____

  b A rectangle measuring 54 mm by 3.5 cm (mm^2)

  _____

  c A rectangle measuring 250 cm by 5 m (m^2)

  _____

  d A rectangle measuring 700 cm by 450 cm (m^2)

  _____

13 This shape is made from rectangles. All measurements are in centimetres.

Find:

  a its perimeter

  _____

  b its area.

  _____

14 How many squares of side 8 cm are needed to cover a rectangle measuring 72 cm by 144 cm?

  _____

15 The shaded triangle is the image of the non-shaded triangle as the result of a translation. Describe the translation.

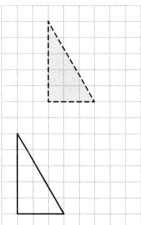

16

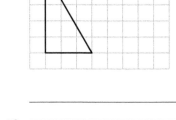

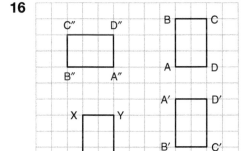

a Which of these shapes is a reflection of rectangle ABCD?

_____

Draw the mirror line.

b Which of these rectangles is the image of ABCD as a result of a translation?

_____

Describe the translation

_____

c A″B″C″D″ is the image of ABCD as a result of a rotation. Mark the centre of rotation with a cross. What is the angle of rotation?

_____

For questions **17** to **22**, which of the shapes have:

a rotational symmetry

b line symmetry

c neither?

17

a _____

b _____

c _____

18

a _____

b _____

c _____

19

a _____

b _____

c _____

20

a _____

b _____

c _____

21

a _____

b _____

c _____

c Find the value of $6 - 3x$ when $x = -2$

_____

d Find the value of x^2 when $x = -4$

_____

27 Solve the following equations:

a $2x - 3 = 7$

_____

b $4x + 3 = 6x - 5$

_____

c $2(x - 3) + x - (5 - x) = 1$

_____

d $5(2x - 1) - 2x = 19$

_____

22

a _____

b _____

c _____

23 Two lengths are in the ratio 5 : 9. The second length is 63 cm. What is the first length?

24 For the set of numbers
24, 85, 8, 5, 20, 5, 55, 75, 83 find:

a the mean

_____

b the mode

_____

c the median

_____

d the range.

_____

25 The mean height of 15 students in a class is 1.57 m. When a new student joins the class the mean height of the students in the class rises to 1.58 m. How tall is the new student?

_____

26 a Simplify $5x + 4(x - 5)$

_____

b Find the value of $3x - 4$ when $x = 3$

_____

28

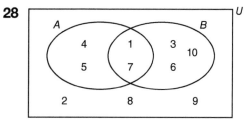

Use this Venn diagram to find:

a A'

_____

b B'

_____

c $A \cup B$

_____

d the complement of $A \cup B$

_____

29

Jamaican dollars	$US	Barbadian dollars	UK pounds (£)
100	0.78	1.65	0.62

Use the exchange rates given in the table to convert:

a 75 000 Jamaican dollars into Barbadian dollars

_____

b 25 000 Jamaican dollars into US dollars

_____

c £744 into US dollars

_____

d £400 into Jamaican dollars

_____

e 800 US dollars into Jamaican dollars

_____

f 500 Barbadian dollars into US dollars

_____

g £350 into US dollars, correct to the nearest $10

_____

h 800 US dollars into £s, correct to the nearest £1.

_____

30 A relation is given by $\{(x, y)\}$ where $y = 20 - x^2$ for $x = 1, 2, 3, 4$.

Complete this table.

x	1	2	3	4
y			11	

31 Find the y-coordinates of the points on the line $y = 2x$ that have x-coordinates of:

a 3 _____

b −2 _____

c 5 _____

d 0 _____

32 Find the x-coordinates of the points on the line $y = -3x$ that have y-coordinates of:

a −1 _____

b $\frac{1}{3}$ _____

c $1\frac{1}{2}$ _____

d 6 _____

33 Express:

a 7500 cm³ in litres

_____

b 3000 mm³ in cm³

_____

c 0.004 m³ in cm³

_____

d 0.025 litres in cm³

_____

34 A rectangular water tank is 2.5 m long, 2 m wide and 1.5 m deep.

a How many litres will it hold?

_____

b If 5000 litres of water is poured into an empty tank, what will be the depth of the water?

_____

c The tank is three-quarters full. 2000 litres is drawn off. How much will the water level sink?

_____

35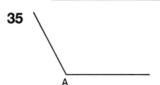

A

Draw any obtuse angle similar to the angle shown above. Label this angle A.

Label the bottom arm of the angle AB, such that AB = 6 cm.

Label the other arm AC such that AC = 6 cm.

Construct the line through C parallel to AB.

Construct the line through B parallel to AC.

Mark D, the point where these two lines cross.

a Measure AC and BD. How do they compare?

_____

_____

b Measure AB and CD. How do they compare?

_____

Join AD and BC. Mark X, the point where they cross.

c Measure angle AXC and angle BXD. How do they compare?

_____

Is this what you expected? Give a reason for your answer.

_____

d What special name do you give for quadrilateral ABCD?

_____

In the remaining questions, choose the letter that gives the correct answer.

36 If –4 is subtracted from 8, and 3 added to the answer, the result is:

A 7   **B** 9

C 11   **D** 15

37 $\frac{0.7}{100}$ has the same value as:

A 0.007%   **B** 0.07%

C 0.7%   **D** 7%

38 Expressed as a percentage, $4\frac{3}{4}$ is:

A 475%   **B** 47.5%

C 4.75%   **D** 0.475%

39 The number of minutes from 9.56 am to 2.15 pm the same day is:

A 186   **B** 199

C 259   **D** 304

40 Expressed in kilograms, 10 lb is approximately:

A $3\frac{1}{2}$ kg   **B** 4 kg

C $4\frac{1}{2}$ kg   **D** 5 kg

41 The value of $\frac{2}{x}+\frac{3}{y}$ when $x = 4$ and $y = 5$ is:

A $\dfrac{9}{10}$ **B** 1

C $1\frac{1}{10}$ **D** $1\frac{1}{5}$

42 The solution of the equation $5x - 7 = 2x + 5$ is $x =$

A 3   **B** 4

C 5   **D** 6

43 How many cubes of side 4 cm will fit into a rectangular carton measuring 24 cm by 16 cm by 8 cm?

A 18   **B** 20

C 24   **D** 48

44 The map ratio of a map is 1 : 200 000. The distance between Esther and Bridport on the map is 4.5 cm. On the ground the distance between these two towns is:

A 8 km   **B** 9 km

C 10 km   **D** 12 km

45 An article which is bought for $6450 and sold for $7224 gives the seller a profit of:

A 10%   **B** 12%

C $12\frac{1}{2}$%   **D** 15%

46 Expressed in litres, 240 000 cm³ is:

A 24   **B** 240

C 2400   **D** 24 000

47 A is a point on the straight line with equation $y = \frac{3}{2}x$
The x-coordinate of A is 6.
Its y-coordinate is:

A 4   **B** 6

C 8   **D** 9

48 A relation is given by $\{(x, y)\}$ where $y = x^2 + x - 6$. When x is 4, the value of y is:

A 2   **B** 14

C 20   **D** 24

49 An article bought for $8400 is sold at a loss of 15%. The selling price is:

A $6300   **B** $6800

C $7140   **D** $9660

50 If 100 Jamaican dollars is equivalent to 0.78 US dollars, the equivalent value of 240 000 Jamaican dollars in US dollars is:

A $1872   **B** $2042

C $2340   **D** $2422

51 The number of square concrete slabs, each of side 40 cm, required to pave a rectangular yard measuring 8 m by 6 m is:

A 280   **B** 300

C 320   **D** 380

UNIVERSITY PRESS

Great Clarendon Street, Oxford, OX2 6DP, United Kingdom

Oxford University Press is a department of the University of Oxford.
It furthers the University's objective of excellence in research, scholarship,
and education by publishing worldwide. Oxford is a registered trade mark of
Oxford University Press in the UK and in certain other countries

Text © Sue Chandler and Ewart Smith 2020
Original illustrations © Oxford University Press 2020

The moral rights of the authors have been asserted

First published by Nelson Thornes Ltd in 2012
This edition published by Oxford University Press in 2020

British Library Cataloguing in Publication Data
Data available

978-0-19-842636-3

10 9 8 7 6 5 4 3 2 1

Printed and bound by CPI Group (UK) Ltd, Croydon, CR0 4YY

Acknowledgements

Cover image: Radachynskyi/iStock

Although we have made every effort to trace and contact all
copyright holders before publication this has not been possible in all
cases. If notified, the publisher will rectify any errors or omissions at
the earliest opportunity.

Links to third party websites are provided by Oxford in good faith
and for information only. Oxford disclaims any responsibility for
the materials contained in any third party website referenced in
this work.